The Lady Persuaders

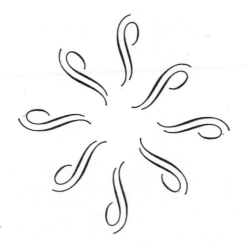

The Lady Persuaders

by HELEN WOODWARD

Ivan Obolensky, Inc.   New York

To my husband W. E. Woodward

Contents

The Lady Persuaders

1

Theme Song

Legally dead. As late as our Civil War, that was the status of a married woman in these United States. Under the law, after the ceremony, the husband was the master of a woman's person and her pocketbook; she had no control over her children; if she earned any money her husband took it over. Sometimes property was settled upon her or was managed by trustees, and in that case her husband could not touch it. In terms of her legal rights, she was classed with a minor, a lunatic or an idiot.

It is a mighty swing from this "legal death"—the words are Blackstone's—to the position of power that women occupied in 1959, when they controlled seventy per cent of the wealth of the country and sometimes wrecked their marriages by earning more money than their husbands. Without their understanding how it all came about, women ruled the roost. They had reached this position through fighting, scratching, screaming, and also through every device of indirection and charm.

In this climb, the women's magazines with their millions of readers played a major part. To the uninitiated, a woman's magazine may seem merely a powdery bit of fluff. No notion could be more unreal or deceptive. That is just the style in which the magazines express themselves, for if the top layer seems fluffy, the underlying base is solid and powerful. These publications involve a giant business investment, and have an overwhelming influence on American life.

I must stop here and confess that I should like very much to find other ways of saying "women's magazines." My secretary suggests "female slicks." That will hardly do. The thesaurus suggests, as substitutes for women, "petticoat" or "weaker vessel." But these are terms that the women's magazines have made obsolete. Like "the distaff side," they have slipped into the past. Since we have no useful word like the French *elles* or the Spanish *ellas,* I shall often use *they,* trusting my readers to understand that I mean a feminine they.

They began small, with their readers in the upper social groups; they grew steadily until they reached most women able to read. Tracing their history, we can make out two steady trends. One is toward democracy, the other toward matriarchal power.

Toward democracy. Maybe Judy O'Grady and the Colonel's lady were sisters under the skin when Kipling wrote about them, but from the skin out they were far apart. Women's magazines have worked hard and successfully to erase this difference.

Toward matriarchal power. Women's magazines have played a major part in bringing about that "Momism" which bothers some theorists and amuses others. They have steadily built up women's authority until it reached the point expressed by the *Ladies' Home Journal* in its slogan, "Never underestimate the power of a woman."

Slowly women took responsibility, dignity and authority away from men. This their magazines encouraged by making Mom and the children play "amusing" tricks on poor, silly Daddy, through cartoons, articles and fiction. The American male was portrayed as a kind of Dagwood Bumstead, likable, lovable, but also foolish, irresponsible, and in need of feminine management. But this propaganda had an unexpected result. Women themselves did not like what was happening in their relations with their husbands and it became important to lure Daddy back into the fold. The downgrading of the man of the family and the upgrading of the woman had gone so far that women became frightened and began to rebel against their power. Their magazines are now testing new conceptions; they are trying to build up the family as a whole; no more rule by either the father or the mother, but a sharing relationship between the two. For the success of such a campaign men also must become readers of the women's magazines. To accomplish this, the *Ladies' Home Journal* used famous writers who the editors thought would appeal to men. But it was *McCall's Magazine* which went furthest, with the slogan "Togetherness," a woefully sad expression, good only for wisecracks. This slogan was really born of fear on the part of the magazines—fear of losing their life's blood—circulation.

Under "Togetherness," man and wife were to share their daily lives in a new and more wholesome fashion. Daddy was to take on more and more household duties. Mom was to take a larger part in his business life. It has been accepted for a long time that women could further their husbands' careers in international diplomacy. Today it is accepted that the wife will help her husband, even direct him, in a political career as well. Her smile and handshake are as important as his. Logically, this has spread into the business world. There is a tendency on the part of big corporations to investigate a man's wife before promoting him to a bigger job. They invite her to parties to see whether she takes too many drinks, if she openly bosses her husband, or if by indirection they can get her to say what she thinks of the firm. In short, they put her under a microscope. Since so many social doings are involved, this whole tendency of the participation of wives increases the effects of snobbery, and so increases the exclusion of able men.

From every point of view this practice seems to me a bad one. It tangles up relationships. Minor disagreements between men can be blown up through their wives into major quarrels. There are other dangers, including the unnecessary strain which such situations can place between husband and wife. But above all, this practice takes away from both men and women the personal privacy to which every individual is entitled. And I should like to sound an alarm. If we don't look out, the first thing we know we'll be following along with the aborigines of South America, among whom, the husband and not the wife used to go to bed after a baby's birth.

But all the campaigns on "Togetherness" and sharing work and pain did not bring circulation back to the magazines. The idea that has leaped over the horizon and brought renewed hope is neither of these, but, as with other industries, it is specialization. *Parents' Magazine* and *Mademoiselle* (an ironic title, since it specializes in young married women between eighteen and thirty) are examples of the success of specialization. It seems odd in the face of such success, that the general women's magazines stick to their old pattern. But it had been a money-making pattern. *Godey's Lady's Book* initiated the basic pattern and followed it from 1828 to 1870. Edward Bok had made changes, and his patterns flourished for two generations. Circulations had sky-rocketed, advertising had flowed.

Then the giants began to fumble. Women had changed, and the very magazines that had once preached the new day were afraid to drop the old methods that had paid off. *Pictorial Review* folded. So did *Delineator* and later, *Woman's Home Companion*.

If for sixty years you have followed certain lines and made huge fortunes out of a policy, you are not going to change it lightly. You will stagger along, mend a spot here, think up a few slogans, do some clever advertising, get some new, startling articles. But you will not throw the whole thing in the wastebasket and start fresh. *Woman's Home Companion* might have saved itself by some such specialization, but preferred to try to hold to the original formula.

Often women's magazines have been foolish, as in their grabbing any new diet notions; sometimes unconsciously comic, as in "Togetherness"; sometimes shocking, as in their recent tasteless handling of sex. Trying to be what the English pronounce "naice," they were sometimes vulgar, but these faults could not destroy the women's magazines. Fundamentally they were sensible and useful. And the word "useful" is the keynote of their history. Successful women's magazines are really trade papers. That is, a woman used to buy them mainly for the technical information she could use. Her job used to be home, husband and children. Today for many, the job has moved out of the house. Some magazine editors have been keen enough to follow this trend, but many have fumbled, trying to guess what the reader really needs or wants.

In the history of these magazines, there were two able, striking people—only two—whose ideas were fresh enough and strong enough to dominate all those who came after them. They were Sarah Josepha Hale and Edward Bok, and the greater of these was Sarah Josepha Hale. Indeed, and I say this with careful thought, I think she was the greatest woman in the history of the country. This book will show why I think so.

The first of "America's female periodicals," *Ladies' Magazine* was born in Boston in 1828. In that same year, Andrew Jackson was elected President of the United States. It did not then occur to anyone that these two events had anything to do with each other, but as we look back, we see that they were indeed part of the same movement, the movement toward democracy. Jackson was the first American President who was not an aristocrat, and from

the very first issue of the *Ladies' Magazine* Mrs. Sarah Josepha
Hale began to work toward democracy. To her, this included power
for women. "Freedom for women" it was called and it was truly
that for a long time. But great movements are apt to move in historical curves, and little by little, *freedom* curved up into *power*.

There is another curious resemblance between Andrew Jackson
and the editors of the women's magazines. For all his belief in democracy, Jackson himself was an autocrat. Sarah Hale and her imi-
tators have been autocrats too. Mrs. Hale was the mother of five
children. Under a soft and beautiful exterior, she was a dominating
woman, a matriarch. She set a pattern of persuasion, flattery, education, polite command, and useful technical information that is
still the basic tool of all women's magazine editors. Mrs. Hale
seems to have had a clear idea of what she was doing. But the editors of the magazines which followed her did not realize what they
were heading for. Often they were snobs, aiming in a different direction, contemptuous of the very audience to which they were
addressing themselves; but they could not help showing their
readers how to look better and how to live better—from the skin
outward anyway.

When Mrs. Hale started her magazine, the husband unquestionably was the head of the family. In harsh Colonial civilization, the
weaker-muscled woman had to take second place. Mrs. Hale taught
her readers to have self-confidence. As a consequence, they changed
the lives of their husbands and children. If we bear this in mind,
we can see clearly a basic difference between magazines for men
and those for women. The women's magazines have always spoken
to their readers as though they were children. They tell their readers what to do; they teach them, they command them, they
threaten and promise them. Men's magazines usually point out,
mention, and explain, but they do not, even in the softest tones,
order their readers to do this and that . . . except in the advertise-

ments. It is because of this difference in psychological approach that the effort to change "Momism" to "Togetherness" was such a tough assignment.

In training their readers, Mrs. Hale and her followers did not try to do too much at once. They went about their campaigns like a woman I know whose little girl doesn't like medicine. She always puts a double dose into the cup or spoon and then she says, "You don't have to take all of it . . . just try a little."

Most of the contents of the women's magazines can roughly be classified under the headings of Entertainment, Enlightenment, Service. The largest part of Entertainment is fiction. For many years it was a mixed bag in quality, mostly sugary and noble and with the invariable happy ending. It followed the sentimental conventions of the period. Details were over-emphasized in an effort to create an illusion of reality. Rupert Hughes, who made a huge success with a long stream of novels, once told me that he owed much of his popularity to careful details. For instance, he said that if his hero and heroine went to a restaurant for lunch, he would be very careful to name the restaurant, say the Hotel Waldorf, give an exact list of what they ate and what they paid for it. This made a good imitation of reality.

A friend of mine, Claudia Cranston, who sold a great many stories to *Good Housekeeping* in the 1920's and 30's, told me that in order to sell these stories, it had been necessary to work out a formula. It took five years of practice before she got it down pat. She says, "In your mind you consider the heroine about forty years old, give her all kinds of experience, sexual and otherwise, have her break all the social rules—and then you describe her as eighteen and pure."

There is still some of that sort of fiction, but, on the whole, it is better than it used to be.

Some of it tries to follow the *New Yorker* pattern for short stories. That pattern avoids drama (does life avoid drama?), is full of meticulous detail and insists on the frustrated ending. While sometimes good, it is often simply long-winded and dull. Other magazines choose their fiction by different means. What they usually do is to get stories of conflict (the *New Yorker* hates conflict) and of course, big names. This fiction branch of their business demands careful study. There are many women who buy the magazines for nothing but the fiction. Women figure this way: if I buy a paperbound book for twenty-five or thirty-five cents, that is all right, but if I pay thirty-five cents for the *Ladies' Home Journal,* I get fiction and some odd bits thrown in. (Funny jokes and verses whose popular theme is the general nuisance of children and the childishness of men.)

On Enlightenment they have come a long way from Mrs. Hale's early efforts, but they have not always come the best way. It may have been a bold stroke to say syphilis out loud, but it was often only a one-copy sale on the newsstand. It took sure instinct on the part of the editors to pick the subjects that would get readers and make them permanent. There has been too much guessing at what the reader might pick off the newsstand and too little trusting the editor's own preference.

It is the Service department which is the backbone of the business. The women's magazines are trade papers for women, just as *Publishers' Weekly* is for the book trade, and *Iron Age* for heavy industry. Naturally features have changed. For instance, reducing diets, which today are sure-fire circulation getters, originally had little place in the magazine. The reason for this is simple. Until fairly recently women did not worry much about their weight. It was accepted that women would be a little plump. Today, women have been scared into starving.

The etiquette department, so popular in earlier days, disappeared for a while. Now it is coming back, though with a different accent to be sure—more easy-going, because more natural.

At first the trade information, i.e., food, dress, etc., was amateurish, written by hit-or-miss guess. There were no real specialists in the field except, of course, those women who ran their own households with assured competence (though most of those could not analyze their methods). With the burgeoning of advertising, the information on such subjects changed. It became a mixture of professional advice and hidden persuasion. When I was in the advertising business in the twenties, I had no trouble at all getting free publicity into the service departments for my clients. Sometimes this publicity was good, as when the Standard Sanitary Corporation pushed their bathrooms and made the United States a clean, cleaner, cleanest nation.

In 1920 women used cotton gingham only in household aprons. Paris dressmakers looked down their noses on cotton goods. One of my customers in Massachusetts manufactured a fine quality of gingham and wanted to make it fashionable. They therefore made up a few bolts of fine gingham in new designs and I went to Paris with them. The fashion magazines *Vogue, Harper's Bazaar,* and the trade magazine *Women's Wear,* gave me almost unbelievable help. They got the *grande couturières* to make clothes of the gingham, found society leaders who would model the dresses, had dolls made and dressed in exact copies. All this was done with large amounts of publicity in the magazines. This sort of publicity seems to me legitimate. This was a good product and the manufacturer was improving his output.

We never approached the advertising men with this material, but went to the editors. Thus the value of the service department was still dependent upon an editorial decision. Oddly, I never tried at that time to get the women's magazines to give us publicity for the books of Mark Twain or O. Henry. This would have been far too remote for the women's magazines, since many of their readers considered these two writers "not quite nice."

These incidents were small potatoes compared to what would go on today, both in the size of the advertising accounts and in the propaganda efforts. As nearly everyone knows, the free publicity business is huge today and highly organized. As a side issue, the guarantees offered by *Good Housekeeping, Parents' Magazine* and *McCall's* work nicely into the free publicity pattern since they are used not only in the magazines which give the guarantees, but also in all sorts of other media, including radio and television. A product called Clairol, which told girls that only blondes could have a good time, announced over television that each of its claims was guaranteed by *Good Housekeeping* and *McCall's*.

Today service departments have a hard time finding material to fill their columns, and the editors search frantically for something to say. There seems little that is new. Millions of new products to do the same old things. Recipes have become more and more warmed over. After all, setting up frankfurters around sauerkraut so that the result looked like a crown roast of lamb could catch the eye only once. Electric stoves and infra-red cooking have helped. Atomic heat will come along. But at the moment it is the deep freeze that fills in.

Most women's magazines now have research departments. Probably *Woman's Day* has the largest and best. But there is some danger that paper and ink and college degrees and wonderful stoves may make us forget that the main thing about food is that it ought to taste good. There is a weary sameness in the recipes which the women's magazines endorse. One reason for the sameness is that many of these household editors have college degrees in home economics, and the courses have a tendency to be more or less alike and are theoretically sterile rather than gustatorily hearty. Since they all have the same sources of information, there is a dull monotony in the text, though there is brilliant variety in the illustrations. Unfortunately, as you turn the pages you often cannot tell which magazine is telling you how to cook what.

Take eggs for example; there is nearly always a recipe for Eggs Benedict, especially after the arrival on the scene of a commercial hollandaise sauce. Then, endlessly, there are the innumerable recipes for omelets. The French are shocked by our frequent addition of water or milk to the eggs. According to the best French recipe, you beat the eggs, not separated, with a fork slightly, melt sweet butter in a heavy pan, pour the eggs in and shake the pan gently until the omelet is ready to be folded over. This is the basic French recipe, but how many times can a magazine repeat anything so simple? So some nonsense has to be added. Bigger and wetter omelets are the result.

During the 1940's competition from radio and television grew sharper. Household information, through repetition and a poverty of new material, was often foolish. Having nothing to say, they continued to say it in more clever and obscure ways.

Then some magazines turned to specialization and sex. By specialization they appealed to separate groups of women. By a profuse use of sex, they aimed at the newsstands.

Financially they are not as well off as they were, but they continue to have a powerful influence on millions of women. They have used this influence often to flatter their readers, to order them and to indoctrinate them. Unfortunately, they have carried this over into new fields: politics, social service, education and, alas, sex. The result is so confused and absurd that a woman who takes them seriously must find herself running in all directions at once. Originally, the magazines had aimed at teaching women how to run the family; now they are teaching them how to run the world.

In these efforts women's magazines avoid arithmetic. They do not touch on such things as the national debt; they avoid the subject of foreign trade. They teach the women to be sympathetic and sorry for all kinds of people, but do not remind them that they must pay for their sympathy through increased income taxes. Political parties, especially those which do not at the moment have a glamour boy as a candidate, are worried about the women's vote. They find it unpredictable because it is apt to be based on whim, and seldom on ideas or principles. The leaders of the New York State A.F. of L. and C.I.O. in 1959 set up a special action division. Its main function was to educate the wives, sisters, mothers, daughters and sweethearts of union members on labor's political objectives. The union officials said that before this they had not been able to get the women to support their candidates or their issues, even though these issues were closely related to wages, prices and the cost of living.

But no matter how tedious and confused the magazine propaganda is, one object is clear. To pull down the man and to uplift the woman, to make the man more feminine and the woman more masculine. In this the women's magazines perfectly represent their times.

2

The Lady

On a Monday, over a century ago, in the City of Troy, New York, Mrs. Hannah Montague got tired of washing all of her husband's shirts when only the collars were soiled. She got tired of carrying heavy tubs of water to the fire. She got even more tired of ironing with the heavy sadirons that she heated on a trivet in her fireplace. So, in the year 1825, Mrs. Montague got out her scissors, cut off the collars, and washed them by themselves. That is how detachable collars were born.

This simple idea would have been welcome to many a woman in the twenty-three states of the Union. The thirteen million people in the United States were spread over wide areas, with vast spaces in between. Though Cincinnati, for instance, was already a well-grown city, it took five days, two ferries, an omnibus, a train and a portage to reach it from New York. Therefore, unless a woman happened to know Mrs. Montague or one of her friends, she would hardly have heard about the new, detachable collars. How could she? There was a Post Office, but there were no envelopes, no adhesive postage stamps, no money orders, no telegraph.[1]

Even if there had been an efficient postal delivery, there was no publication to print such an item as Mrs. Montague's detachable collars. The almanacs and chapbooks were for men, with only gallant and condescending side glances at the ladies. Their only help came from casual bits in the almanacs, used as fillers between more important items about the weather, farming and fortune-telling.

Into this vacuum stepped two people, Louis Antoine Godey and Sarah Josepha Hale. The thin, small-type, prim pamphlet they brought out became the mother of all the giant women's magazines which have changed and are still changing the lives of our people, and of many people throughout the world. In 1828, Mrs. Hale began to edit the *Ladies' Magazine* in Boston. Two years later, Godey started his *Lady's Book* in Philadelphia. Louis Antoine Godey was more successful financially, and, though a poor editor himself, he was quick to recognize Mrs. Hale's editorial ability. She began to help him to select and prepare material for his magazine, but she remained in Boston and continued to edit the *Ladies' Magazine*. Finally, in 1837 Godey bought the *Ladies' Magazine* and combined it with *Godey's Lady's Book*. Mrs. Hale moved to Philadelphia and became the Lady Editor.

There was a lot of "Lady" in all this, but it was the custom of

[1] The first United States Post Office had been established in 1786. But adhesive stamps did not come into existence until 1847. The first stamps were one for five cents with a head of Franklin and one for ten cents with a head of Washington. Before that, you gave the required amount of cash to the Post Office, where your letter would be marked "paid," either in ink or with a stamp. Sometimes the name of the town and the date were added. Often, however, the postage was paid by the recipient. The magazine publishers preferred this method, since the deliveries to subscribers and their credit were both uncertain. Envelopes for letters did not come into use until 1839. The writer simply folded the paper, wrote the address on the back and sealed it with wax.

the time. The word woman was considered an insult; it was used only for sinners and slaves. (This usage persisted for a long time; in 1900 there were still salesladies and washladies.) Still, there had to be a generic word for the sex and that word was "females." If a female wasn't a lady, she had no dignity. The suffrage movement first gave dignity to the word woman although, much earlier, there were some indications of a changing attitude. Richard Henry Dana, distinguished member of a distinguished family, thought the excessive use of "Lady" vulgar.

There was little democracy in the United States in 1828. Not all men had the suffrage. Only eight years had passed since Massachusetts in 1820 had given the vote to male citizens if they paid a poll tax. New York did not give the vote to all white males until 1826 and Rhode Island and Virginia were the only states which did not require a religious qualification for voters and office holders. A property qualification for voting was common. The right of suffrage was restricted to people of property, except in New Hampshire, Pennsylvania and Georgia. In those states any free white male resident might qualify as a voter by paying a poll tax.

The kind and variety of suffrage restrictions of that period will perhaps surprise most people unfamiliar with the political history of our country. In Maryland a voter had to own fifty acres of land or possess thirty pounds in money. In 1790 in New York State, only 1209 men out of 340,000 were qualified to vote for a state senator. In New York, too, niggling distinctions were not abolished until 1826: A man had to own one hundred pounds to vote for a state senator; if he owned twenty pounds he could vote for a member of the lower house. In New Jersey he could vote if he owned fifty pounds. At first females also could vote in New Jersey with the same proviso, but before 1828 this female right was abolished. Even veterans of the revolution fell under the ban of these qualifications. Tennessee was one of the last states to remove a property qualification for voters. In 1810, South Carolina abolished the property qualification for the vote and granted the suffrage to every white male, but Connecticut held to the property and religious qualification as a basis for suffrage.

It isn't generally known that the Fourteenth Amendment was the first in the United States Constitution to give the vote to all white males, as well as to all others regardless of race. Before this time, many states had restrictions on sections of their white voters.

There were few public schools. The idea of universal education was unwelcome. Taxpayers refused to contribute money for the benefit of other people's children. In New York, for example, the well-to-do paid fees for their children and the poorer felt they had to do the same, since to refuse would make them appear to be paupers. The alternative was to keep their children at home. The teaching profession (a kind of vagabond and impoverished existence) was regarded with contempt until, in 1827, Horace Mann and Henry Barnard started campaigns which made teaching more reputable. After that it became a mixed picture; some teachers were still itinerant; the lady teachers of dame schools were highly respectable. At that time, half the women in the country could not read, much less write. Glimmers began to appear; Noah Webster's Speller sold 5,000,000 copies, McGuffey's Reader came out in 1836.

Massachusetts was the most enlightened state about child labor. In 1836, that Commonwealth passed a law specifying that all children under fifteen had to attend school at least three months a year.

When Sarah Josepha Hale brought out her first issue in 1828, the street crossings of New York were swept by homeless little boys and girls. Even if such a little girl could have cleaned herself up, there was a social gap as wide as the Grand Canyon between her and the little girl whose governess held her by the hand as she crossed the street. Of course, there are plenty of women working right now at cleaning up for other people, but when such a woman gets dressed up, she looks and feels as good as the next one. Dressing up may be an example of "conspicuous waste" but the satisfaction it gives a woman is not a waste. Quite the contrary, it gives her self-confidence.

If a working woman in Mrs. Hale's early days had had anything in the way of money to waste, conspicuously or otherwise, she would have been rather remarkable. In that day New England factories sent out covered wagons called "slavers" to entice girls from the farms to work in the mills. The slavers promised to give the girls silk dresses and to teach them how to read. The girls worked for a dollar a week and board. Data on the silk dresses is unavailable, but since the girls worked from twelve to fourteen hours a day, they probably didn't need silk dresses. Baths were not mentioned in the *Ladies' Magazine*. Apparently, they were not considered important. Even the fine folk were not over-clean. The first running-water bathtub in a private house was not installed until 1832 (the year Sarah Josepha Hale began to help Godey with his magazine). Thereupon, Boston passed an ordinance making it a crime to use a tub, perhaps because it implied nakedness, though the excuse was that the tub was a danger to health. Some women bathed in their nightgowns, which sounds rather hazardous and inconvenient. One of the early issues of Godey's magazine told the ladies to be careful to wash their ears, and gave detailed instructions. This, remember, was for the highest social circles.

The whole toilet of the ear consists in paying proper attention to cleanliness. Externally the concha or external cavities are to be washed and carefully dried.

On the delicate subject of the feet, the *Lady's Book* said:

It is necessary, especially in hot weather, to wash the feet frequently, as they perspire much and are more exposed to dust, than any other part of the human frame. The water should be warm, but not too much so because hot water, when used, relaxes the fibers, drives the blood upwards, and occasions headaches. The proper degree of heat for young persons to wash in is between 96 and 98 of Fahrenheit; and, for the aged, somewhat more lukewarm.

And repulsive from our point of view was one which told how "to remove the black dye left on the skin from wearing mourning in warm weather."

Other methods for keeping clean were even less attractive. In 1845, when elegance called for a dinner of fourteen courses, Philip Hone, ex-Mayor of New York, a wealthy man who entertained the important visitors to the city, remarked in his famous diary on the use of "finger glasses":

I think it unseemly to see a company at the dinner table, particularly the female part, washing their hands, rubbing their gums with the fingers, and squirting the polluted water back into the vessel, as was formerly the fashion in this country, a fashion which yet prevails in England in the higher circles.

Mrs. Montague, who cut off the collars of her husband's shirts, was a middle-class woman. When she dressed up in her best, you could tell at once her place in the hierarchy of caste. You would not for a moment confuse her with a "great lady," nor would you take her for one of those pioneer women who lived in sod houses on the prairies.[2] A woman like Mrs. Montague would perhaps get

---

[2] Sod houses were built around 1830 where timber was scarce. Turf was cut into three-inch bricks. Roofs of sod were laid on poles. Over this roof was spread a layer of prairie grass, from which sunflowers often blossomed.

a new dress once every ten years. Either she made it herself or had a local seamstress do the best she could from a picture. Much of this sewing was done by farm women during the winter months. As the gowns then in fashion were fussy with ruffles and ribbons and lace and what not, the copy could not be mistaken for the original. All the sewing was done by hand. The sewing machine had not yet been invented. The pioneer woman wore what she could get, sometimes made from a sack, sometimes from good solid material which she wove herself. And she used it for a lifetime.

As for the wealthy woman, she would send a mold of her body to London, and when she needed a new costume, have a pattern cut out there. This was usually made either of cheap cloth to be shipped to America and worked up at home or it was cut into the material of the actual dress.

In an early issue of *Godey's* there is an announcement that a pattern would be cut in cheap material but in the actual colors of the final dress. The number of colors was limited and their lasting power uncertain. Chemical discoveries are responsible for the vast and fast variety now used.

The nation as a whole was coarse and raw. Cruelty and brutality caused little comment. The Revolutionary War had left the country in a chaotic moral state, without adequate police or just laws. The countryside was plagued with robbery and rape. People were hanged for small thefts. Wife beating carried no stigma. During the Colonial period, children were sold, white as well as black. Some of these white children had committed small crimes in England, the penalty for which was death, so that it was actually as a humanitarian measure that the children were shipped to America as indentured servants, sometimes for a period of years, sometimes for life. With the establishment of the independence of the Republic, this practice was outlawed. But consciences were hardened toward indentured servants, and the practice, though less, lingered on. Sometimes the very poor who could not support their children used it too.

The debtors' laws in New York were the harshest in the Union; imprisonment, even for small sums, was common. But even in Boston in 1820, thirty-five hundred were still so imprisoned, and of these five hundred were women. This is surprising, since a married woman could not borrow money except as her husband's agent. Confusion in the laws of the different states encouraged crimes, which were much more numerous in proportion to the population than they are today. Much of the confusion in the laws was foolish and unnecessary. Other laws, seemingly ridiculous, had a reasonable foundation. For instance, in Massachusetts it was legal to dig for clams, but not to dredge for oysters. (Clams were in heavy supply there; oysters were scarce.)

Away from the thin line of coastal cities, the men were rough-bearded and usually carried revolvers. Earlier historians commented on their wearing coarse jeans, but, now, in the long swing of history the wearing of jeans has become a mark of social nonchalance. Although law and law enforcement agencies were not as well founded in the interior as in the seaports, and although men in the interior relied more heavily on their personal ability to protect themselves, history has greatly exaggerated these differences. In the matter of drunkenness, there was no distinction between the coast cities and the interior; men got drunk in both areas. They were not expected to "hold their liquor." The amount of rum and whiskey a man could consume before he went to rest under the table was astounding.

As a reaction to the roughness that existed on all sides, speech among gentlefolk was prudish. Noah Webster set out to edit the Bible to get rid of its naughty words. He changed "go whoring" to "go astray," "give suck" to "nurse," "cockroach" to "roach," "go to bed" to "retire," and "sows" to "female hogs." Legs, of course, did not exist; they were "limbs," and a gentleman did not mention a shirt in the presence of ladies.

Louis Antoine Godey went along with all this; he did nothing to offend the prudishness and fastidiousness of his readers. Even Sarah Hale seemed, if read hastily, to put women into straight-jackets. Actually, in spite of these restrictions, Mrs. Hale managed to proselytize steadily for the education of women. Yet she did so while adroitly avoiding such block-busting issues of her day as slavery and abolition, or even woman suffrage.

Everyone who writes of Louis Antoine Godey begins by saying that he looked like Mr. Pickwick. Maybe he did. He was a round, small, plump man, but he never would have fallen victim to Mrs. Bardwell. He was willing to stake a good deal on his enthusiasms, but he was a shrewd man who knew his limitations. He published *Godey's Lady's Book* for forty-seven years and made a large fortune from it. But he would never have achieved this if he had not seen and admired the little magazine which Sarah Josepha Hale was editing in Boston.

Godey was thirty-seven years old, a man of open mind, untrammeled by education, when he began to issue *Godey's Lady's Book* in Philadelphia. He had no central plan for it; he merely threw it together, a ragbag of scraps he thought women would like, a sort of catch-all. The word magazine originally meant storehouse, and Godey abided by that meaning, storing up anything that came along. Sometimes he hit it right; sometimes wrong. But his principal strength and success was simply that he had no competition. For his first article he chose fashion news from England, and, as a forepiece, a beautiful hand-colored fashion plate that is a collector's item today. These fashion plates were featured in each issue and were the real prize in *Godey's*. The artist added a personal touch for the subscribers by using variety in his hand coloring. Mrs. Jones had her coloring in yellow and mauve, while Mrs. Brown's was in pink and green.

There was little lightness or humor in the *Lady's Book*. Mr. Godey himself was jolly, affable, but the tone of the magazine was somber and earnest. In an early issue, a story entitled "Leper's Confession" began with the words: "The curse of Heaven is upon me." The whole tendency in Godey's magazine was toward deep gloom. There was a great deal about suicides. One piece, dark indeed, was called "The Last Carouse." High moral tone, of course.

Most of his material was clipped from English publications without acknowledgment, as there was no copyright agreement between the two countries. In this kind of infringement, Godey was no different from other American publishers of his time who brought out Dickens, Thackeray, Scott and others without permission or royalty payment. Much of the material in the *Lady's Book* was unsigned, or, if the author was a woman, might be signed with a male pseudonym. This habit of using a pseudonym or "anonymous" went on for many years. *The Encyclopaedia Britannica* states that "A Lady" was signed to more than a thousand separate works. Edgar Allan Poe's *Tamerlane* (in 1827) was signed "A Bostonian."

On the whole, Godey's material was cheaper and cruder than Sarah Hale's Boston paper. She chose her material with care, always bearing in mind her basic purpose, that she would make every reader a lady and that she would instill in her, cautiously, the desire for improvement, for education and freedom.

The attitude of the man in the family was one roadblock for Mrs. Hale. The father ruled absolutely, in theory anyway. He was, it seems, in deadly fear lest his wife should get to know something that would make her his equal. One wonders if there wasn't some kind of weakness in this attitude. Naturally, such a relationship did not exist among settlers in the new territories, where a man and his wife shared rough work. Even on the frontier, however, the husband controlled the property and the wife was "legally dead." But it was in the cities, in the middle and upper classes that the restrictions upon women were most severe. It was the high-toned lady who had to ask her husband's permission for everything she did. Jane Austen's heroes and Jane Eyre's Mr. Rochester were men like that.

Mrs. Hale handled this situation with the finest velvet over her iron hand. In 1828 she wrote:

Husbands may rest assured that nothing found in these pages shall cause her (his wife) to be less assiduous in preparing for his reception or encourage her to "usurp station" or encroach upon the prerogatives of men.

As a further sop to the male Cerberus, Mrs. Hale, in 1838, wrote:

To excel them in wit men find is the most difficult to pardon in women. This feeling, if it produce only emulation, is right . . . if envy, it is wrong. For a high degree of intellectual refinement in the female is the surest pledge society can have for the improvement of the male. But wit in women is a jewel, which, unlike all others, borrows lustre from its setting, rather than bestows it; since nothing is so easy as to fancy a very beautiful woman extremely witty.

Mrs. Hale had a clear idea of what she wanted in a magazine, and the pattern she set endures to this day. She was a fighting feminist, but a feminist in veil, silks and kid gloves. She combined in herself two seemingly opposite qualities which appealed to her readers. She pleaded for, worked for, fought for the education of women. But she was sentimental too. (It is said that she wrote "Mary Had A Little Lamb.")

If Mr. Godey looked like Mr. Pickwick, Mrs. Hale looked like Dora Copperfield. But she was as unlike Dora as he was unlike

Pickwick. She was a little woman, so slender she seemed tall, a beautiful creature who all her life dressed to look useless, which was the ideal for the ladies of her youth. Her blue eyes sparkled under a high, broad forehead. A straight nose, sensitive lips, pink and white complexion, made a model of beauty for her followers. But inside her pretty little head was a disciplined and muscular mind.

Sarah Josepha Buell was born in Newport, New Hampshire, on October 24, 1788, a year before George Washington was elected President. There were no colleges or even first class academies for women. But she was fortunate that her brother Horatio, one year older than she, was a student at Dartmouth. He taught her mathematics, Latin and what she called mental philosophy. At eighteen, she started a simple school for small children which she kept going for seven years in her father's house. Women were not given real teaching jobs. They taught in dame schools, with all the fancy ruffles of education, or, like the one Sarah ran, small schools for the very young.

Usually these schools were not as good as the kindergartens of today, but Sarah Hale's was better. She refused to bother her pupils with sewing, but taught them how to write and read for pleasure, and she gave them more mathematics than was expected.

When she was twenty-five and already considered a confirmed spinster, she met and married David Hale, a brilliant young lawyer from a nearby town. This was in the year 1813. The war of 1812 was taking its foolish course, but, in the back country of New Hampshire, the war was hardly felt.

It was a radiantly happy marriage. Sarah bore her husband five children in their nine years together. David Hale was a hard working lawyer, and Sarah needed most of her time and energy for her children. Life in the little New Hampshire town was bare of outside events, but simple things could be dramatic as when a wagon drove up, unloaded men and straw, and proceeded to make bricks from the native soil. With these bricks they put up shaky but beautiful houses we still come across in the countryside of Vermont and New Hampshire.

Sarah and David had lively minds, and together they always found ways to keep their minds busy. They were the kind of people who got restless when their minds were not working. Together they studied French, botany, mineralogy and geology. He gave her confidence in her own powers of mind, and he was, she said, abler than she in every quality except imagination.

Sarah Hale was not physically strong. After she had had two babies and a third baby was on the way, she got tuberculosis. Her sister Martha had died young from the same cause and Sarah seemed doomed, since the disease was common in New England, and at the time meant a sentence of death. Her husband, however, would not believe that tuberculosis had to be fatal. Far ahead of his time, he declared that fresh air was a cure for the disease.

Many years later she told her granddaughter, Sarah Hale Hunter, how David had cured her:

"It was the fall of the year, and the grapes were ripe. One evening your grandfather had been reading aloud to me as I reclined on the sofa, when right in the middle of a sentence he suddenly closed the book and walked out of the house without a word. He was gone a long time. Where he went or what he did he never told me. But when he came back he picked me up in his arms. 'Listen,' he said, 'you are not going to die. I won't *let* you.'

"The very next morning he and I started on a trip through the mountains in a gig. For six days we drove every day; it was delightful weather; and I ate grapes. We had heard of the grape cure and your grandfather decided to try it. Also he had a theory that fresh air ought to be good for sick lungs. The doctor vowed David would never bring me home alive, but David did bring me home, cured."

Mrs. Hunter goes on:

"To the end of her life, Mrs. Hale ate grapes; always on the table in her room she kept a plate of grapes. When they were out of season, she paid unheard of prices for the hot-house kind." [3]

But David Hale, who had saved Sarah, could not save himself. They had been married only nine years when he died of pneumonia. Sarah grieved for him all the years of her long life. As far as she could, she tried to keep the details of her appearance like those that had pleased him. Though she was sensitive to fashion, she always wore her hair in the side curls David had admired— whether they were in or out of style.

Sarah Hale Hunter writes that her grandmother seldom spoke of her husband, but on the anniversary of their marriage, she would tell stories about him, how handsome he had been, how kind, and how much beloved by his friends.

In the year of his death, she had little time to grieve. There were five children, the oldest seven, and the youngest a boy born two weeks after his father died. Sarah had no money. She had no training for making a living, or providing for a family of six. She had only the hard and basic mental training begun by her brother Horatio and continued by her husband. Teaching would not bring in enough. Instead, she tried the obvious occupation of her day—millinery. She was a dismal failure. But, at last, the door to her great future opened a little way. She wrote a novel, and at first she could not get a publisher. However, the Order of Freemasons, to which her husband had belonged, stepped in and paid for its publication. Her novel was not important as literature, but it attracted attention and brought in needed dollars. It also expressed many of her

[3] *The Lady of Godey's* by Ruth E. Finley.

revolutionary opinions. Some of these showed keen historical fore-
sight. For instance, in 1828 she already saw that there might be
a war between the States and that it would be due to economic
causes rather than to a struggle over slavery. Such opinions, so
frankly expressed in her novel, she kept under wraps for a long
time after she became a magazine editor.

A Boston firm, admiring her novel, offered to start a magazine
for her; so she moved herself and her five children to Boston. She
was forty years old and she had no training for the new work. She
was afraid—for this was to be a magazine for women—and there
was no other such periodical to consult or follow.

In all this she never forget that she was a woman and a beauty.
Every night she put strips of heavy wrapping paper wet with vine-
gar to her forehead to keep off crow's feet. She concocted a hand
lotion of lard, rose water, and cocoanut milk which was her only
other cosmetic. A high Episcopalian, she went religiously to
church. Dressed for that occasion, people said she looked like a
duchess, walking straight and fast on her tiny feet.

She had a housekeeping instinct and hated disorder. To the end
of her days she was bothered by a dropped pin. This was partly
superstition, but it was also left over from her young days when
pins were made by hand and cost five cents each.

Her admirers made her out an angel, while others thought her a
ruthless feminist. The truth is that she was a good woman who
wanted to make other people better. Considering herself fortunate
in having had a husband who had respected her intelligence and
imagination, she wanted other women to have this same advantage,
and thus she had much to do with shaping the destiny of the
American family.

The self-educated Godey and the highly educated Sarah Hale
began to join forces in 1832. Godey was not financially successful
until then, when he got Mrs. Hale to work with him. He wanted

her as a full-time editor. In order to get her to come to Philadelphia, he bought her Boston magazine. But the strong-willed lady said she would not go until her eldest son had graduated from Harvard. She kept Godey waiting for four years while the young man finished his education. She then moved to Philadelphia with all her five children. She became the full-time editor of the combined magazine, which from then on became known as *Godey's Lady's Book*. Able as they were, neither Antoine Godey nor Sarah Hale dreamed that in the life of the American family they were starting a revolution.

The price of *Godey's Lady's Book* was three dollars a year. In buying power that would be equal to at least twelve dollars today. There was no competition. Each copy was, no doubt, read by a whole group of friends, who often shared the expense. There was no arrangement for prepaid postage. Subscriptions were taken by agents; mail efforts were either non-existent or too small to notice. I have not been able to find out what commissions the agents received. No doubt they varied. The magazines were shipped in bulk to these agents who paid the postage, and if they could, collected it from the subscribers. There were no circulation schemes or premiums. There was no advertising.

The size of the magazine varied a good deal, but an issue of 1830 was about the average; it measured six by nine inches, set in two columns of small type on rag paper, and was usually about thirty-two pages. There was no formal table of contents. Sometimes there was a sheet of music. Nearly all the readers of *Godey's* could read music at sight much better than they could read books; most of them played the piano or organ. This habit of giving sheet music within magazines and Sunday papers lasted until the coming of records and phonographs. I remember when I was a child in Little Rock, Arkansas, we waited eagerly for the Sunday paper from St. Louis because it included a sheet of music.

Mrs. Hale did not take over the combined magazines completely until 1837. Even then, she kept herself in the background and merely signed herself, "The Lady Editor." Yet, except for reprints from British magazines, she wrote nearly everything in the publication. Since there was no advertising to fill space, this was a sizeable job.

Mrs. Hale did not like the custom of using material without copyright or permission. In the 1840's, she began to acknowledge and to pay writers for their work. This did not make her at all popular with other publishers; they attacked her for it bitterly. But Antoine Godey gave her his full support. From the time she took over, until 1870, she remained the editor, without interference. Her decisions were final and unquestioned. For his part, Godey tended to business, to obtaining the materials, the printing and distribution. He was making a handsome profit and had no intention of interfering with the source of the golden eggs.

There is no point in giving an exhaustive list of the contents of the magazine, for through the years of the eighteen thirties and forties the basic contents of the magazine were about the same in every issue.

There was a good deal of space given to avoiding sunburn. A red or tanned skin was a sign that their possessor labored, and we all know how degrading it was for women to work with their hands at that time (except at sewing a fine seam without pay). The sun-tan for which people work so hard today would have thrown Godey's women readers into unacceptable social darkness.

Mrs. Hale recommended this "Fine Wash for Any Redness in the Face: Boil two ounces of barley, two ounces of blanched almonds to a paste, mix them with a little of the barley water. When cold, warm them and squeeze them through a cloth; then dissolve a penny worth of camphor in a tablespoonful of brandy or any strong spirits. Mix them together, and wash the face with the liquid every night when going to bed." This, says the original recipe, "is the best wash ever made for the face."

She thought that the goose quill was in better taste and more practical than the steel pen, "for the lady who is seldom employed at her escritoire,[4] the silver and steel pens have always seemed to us to be hard and unpleasant," she wrote. There followed twelve hundred words on how to keep a goose-quill pen in shape (and it required as much care as a baby) and how to write politely.

Of course there were no typewriters. To the editors of today, the thought of editing a manuscript written in longhand is nightmarish. It seems incredible to the modern writer that Dickens and Thackeray wrote their long novels by hand and, worse, that they corrected those handwritten manuscripts. All those novels might have been shorter (though perhaps not better) if there had been a typewriter. Balzac rewrote and edited his books after they were set in type in galleys—a very expensive process indeed.

Nevertheless, in spite of handicaps, the standards of fiction in America were improving. England was producing some of her finest literature and the novel was in full bloom. *Godey's Lady's Book* followed this trend, and began also to discover the best of the American writers. For instance, Mrs. Hale bought a great deal from Edgar Allan Poe.

Her basic purpose, however, remained unchanged. From the very first issue Sarah Hale strove toward achieving her own image of the American woman. She coaxed rather than fought, for she herself was a lady. She coaxed and under the coaxing was the command, the sweet and gentle, unrelenting command. She considered the toilet (now toilette) of paramount importance to women, but she always liked to put in a word for her higher goal. "Although the toilet should never be suffered to engross so much of the attention as to interfere with the higher duties of life, yet, as

[4] French words indicated elegance.

a young lady's dress, however simple, is considered a criterion of her taste, it is, certainly, worthy of her attention. Her chief object in this respect should be to acquire sufficient skill and good taste to do all that is needful, with regard to attire, in the least possible period of time . . . to abbreviate the labours of the toilet so as not to encroach upon hours which should be devoted to the useful avocations of life, or the embellishments of the mind."

Thus was set the pattern for what the American woman was to become. But progress was slow. There can be no doubt that the whole woman's suffrage movement was slowed up by the hideous clothes and unattractive appearance of its early leaders. Mrs. Carrie Chapman Catt was one of the first among the suffragettes who was both handsome and well dressed. She wore her white hair carefully waved. But this was not until after 1912. Before that time, the women in the suffrage movement had never understood Sarah Hale's belief that a woman's power was not through direct competition with men, but by proving, as she said, that they were able to retain all their most attractive feminine traits and, at the same time, take part in the "useful avocations of life."

3

Fighting with Feather-Duster Prose

Sarah Josepha Hale was by temperament a user of what the *New Yorker's* John McCarten once described as feather-duster prose. She combined flattery, advice, command, all soft and feathery. That has been the pattern of women's magazines ever since, never quite hitting on the dirty spot, but flipping at it.

But Sarah Hale's *ideas* were not in the least feathery. Her ideas were clear and she was a fighter. Still she cut her purpose to suit her public and wrapped it in cotton wool for them. Her ideas about politics were definite but, on the whole, she kept them out of the *Lady's Book*. She knew that gentlemen did not like their wives to think about such things. Even more than that, she believed that her readers did not know enough to make proper political judgments.

She never lifted a pen for woman's suffrage. When she began to edit the *Ladies' Magazine* in 1828, the first suffrage association was being formed. She did not mention it. In 1850 when Elizabeth Cady Stanton was the leader of the movement, when the newspapers were full of the subject, Sarah remained cold to it. This is what she said at that time in *Godey's Lady's Book:*

We have said little of the Rights of Women. But her first right is to education in its widest sense, to such education as will give her the full development of all her personal, mental and moral qualities. Having that, there will be no longer any questions about her rights; and rights are liable to be perverted to wrongs when we are incapable of exercising them.

Mrs. Hale certainly condescended to her readers, and condescension is still noticeable in the women's magazines of today. Reading them, one must conclude that their editors are either silly and muddled, or else contemptuous of their subscribers.

But if Mrs. Hale condescended to her readers, she respected the potentialities of women. From the day she took charge of *Godey's,* she put women in every possible job on the *Lady's Book,* and by her example led other publishers to increase the number of women on their staffs. "The *Lady's Book* was the first avowed advocate of the holy cause of woman's intellectual progress; it has been the pioneer in the wonderful change of public sentiment prospecting female education and the employment of female talent in the teaching of the young." [1]

In short, Sarah was a fighting feminist but there was no votes-for-women about her. Education should come first; then the vote. And suffrage actually did come before women were properly educated for it. We can now see how right Mrs. Hale was. But her wisdom was ignored. Women without adequate knowledge have used the suffrage to meddle in politics and society. For knowledge they have substituted a vague "kind-heartedness." They often know how to manipulate Parliamentary Rules, and do so even when they know practically nothing about history, geography or economics. They

[1] From *The Lady of Godey* by Ruth E. Finley.

know how to bring pressure through lobbies, even though they take part only because a "best friend" asked them to sign up.

This may sound as though I think women should not have the vote. No indeed. They should. Only I hate to see the privilege misused and abused by bright women who refuse to use their brains. If education means tough mental training, I am for it, a lot more of it than we have.[2]

Mrs. Hale was ahead of her time in her theories for bringing up children. In her first magazine in Boston, she ran a section called "Letters from a Mother" which was really a department of child psychology. She advocated schools for infants, a sort of predecessor to the modern nursery school, but with much more mental training than small children get today. But she did think that, in the presence of adults, children should be seen and not heard. It is therefore surprising that Mrs. Hale was against corporal punishment at home and even more so in schools. This was absolutely revolutionary at the time, but she spoke with the authority of a woman who had brought up five children with fine results. She said "nothing can be more absurd than the attempt to break the temper and crush the will . . . while of all debasing, degrading influences, the worst is bodily fear."

It isn't fair to look down on *Godey's Lady's Book* for the things that its editors could not know at the time. It was the custom to feed babies on coffee pap, on sips of beer and hard cider, and to put them to sleep with paregoric. We can hardly blame Sarah Josepha Hale or her readers because they did not know about vitamins, which hadn't been discovered, although cider did contain a lot of

---

[2] Today the president-elect of a woman's club must be pretty. She should wear small hats which should be off the face. The members are likely to vote for her because "she's a darling." But what she really has to be is a strong politician. As for their larger votes on the political scene, the members are likely to say: "I just love him," or "I can't bear him," or in private, "He can put his shoes under my bed anytime."

Vitamin C. Altogether, Sarah Hale was the equal of any man of her time in power of personality and quality of mind. She was a teacher in the kindergarten of the grown-up woman's world. That world, when it could afford it, wore crinolines and corsets on its minds as well as its bodies. Sarah Hale did her best to strip the ruffles and stiffenings from women's thoughts and spirits.

She had a heavy load of work in Boston. Besides editing the magazine she had to bring up her five children, and while she was a careful and intelligent mother, yet she managed to leave enough energy and enthusiasm for the creation of new public movements. She surprised her contemporaries by the number of these enterprises, enterprises quite different from the usual charitable do-goods of her period. They were more in the line of social planning, which was a new and unexplored field in the thinking of that day. Some of her ideas were so far ahead of her time that they did not come into fruition until more than many years later, long after she had died.

The first of her efforts was purely patriotic. It was to raise money for a monument at Bunker Hill, which shocked the men of her times, because it was being done by a woman. Bostonians (male) had started on the project in 1822; Daniel Webster praised it, Lafayette came and spoke for it, and then it petered out and wound up in a pile of granite blocks strewn helter-skelter over Breed's Hill.[3] And there it lay for eight years. In 1830, Mrs. Hale took hold with her usual high spirits. She was genuinely moved by the idea of the monument, and, in addition, it did no harm to the circulation of the *Ladies' Magazine*. She organized ten women of social importance in Boston. But her magazine was small, its editorials had little influence and all she was able to raise was $3,000. But it had this distinction; it came a single dollar each,

[3] The monument known as Bunker Hill is really on another hill known as Breed's.

from 3,000 women, and even though the ladies had to get their dollars from their husbands who scoffed at the effort, nonetheless this was the first all-women's money-raising effort made exclusively by women.

But again the project languished, this time for ten years, when the group behind the Monument confessed its failure. Again Mrs. Hale took hold, but this time she could do much more, for she had *Godey's Lady's Book* to help out. What she did would not be overwhelming today, but in 1840, it was sensational, and again it was done entirely by women.

She proposed that Boston should have a fair, a woman's fair. And this time the newspapers of New England backed her up. "That summer women . . . knit, crocheted, made patchwork quilts and waxwork, put up jellies, conserves, pickles" [4] . . . not only in Boston but in the South and Middle West. The fair ran seven days in Quincy Hall, in Boston and raised $30,000. Sarah had won. The Monument was finished in 1843, and Sarah was a public figure of importance. And women had shown what they could do.

But meantime, back in 1833, Mrs. Hale had started another project that was really much more important when she conceived and organized the Seaman's Aid Society.

Sarah Hale had gone through five, lean widow's years herself and she understood the penny-pinching day-by-day struggle of the seamen's wives in Boston. Most of the ships still moved under sail, and their voyages for trading and whaling were long. A seaman was away from his family for months, sometimes years. His top pay was eighteen dollars a month and he often had to accept ten or twelve. Out of this he had to use up two months' pay in advance for his equipment and outfitting for the voyage. Mrs. Hale said that this left his family so little that the wife could barely pay for rent and fuel. She had to earn money to support herself and her

[4] Lady of Godey's by Ruth E. Finley.

children and her only means of earning money was to go in service to families or take in washing or needlework.

The Seamen's Aid Society began small. As Mrs. Hale said: "The ladies who assisted carried each month to our meetings a basketful of donations which they called Work Baskets. We passed the afternoon making garments to be given to the poor." And she showed her forward-looking common sense, when she added: "Though the greatest need of most of them was employment." [5]

The Work Basket expanded. By 1836 it had become a clothing store, where seamen's outfits were sold, the garments having been made by wives of sailors. The store was a huge success, but, as might be expected, the keepers of waterfront slop shops and the manufacturers of seaman's outfits started a fight against the Society which backfired. It came out these slop shops were hiring not only women but children, were paying them six cents for making a shirt and ten cents for a pair of trousers. All of these, of course, were sewed by hand.

The Society later opened a trade school for girls which developed into the first day nursery, and still later, a free library. Because of the wretched tenements in which these sailors' families lived, Mrs. Hale began in her magazine to work for model tenements; she tried to have a minimum rent law introduced into the Massachusetts legislature, but this effort failed. The country was far from ready for such ideas and could not even understand what she meant when she talked of "the effects of environment on character."

One of her major campaigns was for Elizabeth Blackwell, who had the then outrageous notion that although she was a woman, she wanted to be a "doctress." "Mad" or "bad" said the astounded press.

It was pretty hard on a woman who was sick; she was too

[5] From *The Lady of Godey* by Ruth E. Finley.

"modest" to let a male doctor examine her. Said one leading doctor, "I am proud to say that in this country, generally women prefer to suffer the extremity of danger and pain, rather than waive the scruples of delicacy." [6]

So, while these ladies would not let a man doctor examine them, they thought that a woman must be shameless to want to examine the intimate parts of the body in a medical class with men. For years, Elizabeth Blackwell had been turned down by every university medical department. Finally, she was accepted by Geneva Medical School in New York and graduated in 1849, the first woman to hold a degree as a Doctor of Medicine. But her fight was far from over. For years she was attacked, and only Sarah Josepha Hale in *Godey's Lady's Book* stood by her. That struggle led Mrs. Hale into her fight against the midwives who were then American Sairy Gamps, drunken, sluttish creatures who killed women and babies by their ignorance and laziness.

Sarah Hale fought so many amazing fights, and accomplished so many things both by herself and through her magazine, that I should like to include a bare list of some of them here: [7]

She was responsible for making Thanksgiving a national holiday.

She was an early champion of elementary education for girls and of higher education for women.

She was the first to advocate women as teachers in the public schools.

As the friend and advisor of Matthew Vassar, she helped organize Vassar College, the first school of collegiate rank for girls.

She demanded for housekeeping the dignity of a profession and put the term "domestic science" into the language.

She began the fight for the retention of property rights by married women.

She founded the first society for the advancement of women's wages,

[6,7] From *The Lady of Godey* by Ruth E. Finley.

better working conditions for women, and the reduction of child labor. Yet she believed that women should take less pay than men for the same work, because otherwise they would not get the work at all. She also believed that they act as scabs in labor disputes.

She was the first to suggest public playgrounds and among the earliest to recognize health and sanitation as civic problems.

She wrote *against* the cinched waist, and for weekly baths, which at that time were regarded as a danger to health.

When the sewing machine was invented she gave it enthusiastic support and much free advertising.

While in some of these undertakings she was ahead of her time, in many of them she was in harmony with the mood of her period. The country was beginning, though in a small way, to fight against imprisonment for debt, for prison reform and similar movements. Fourteen of the states had prohibition laws.

In some areas of the country there were communal experiments like Brook Farms and the Owen Community. Surprising, in view of the "nice Nellyism" of the period, was the acceptance of the Oneida Community with its "Compound Marriage" by which every man was married to every woman in the community and the children belonged to all of them.

There were many quirks in Sarah Hale's thinking. She believed that the solution to the Negro slave problem was to send all Negroes back to Africa. Although in the 1830's Congress was turbulent with fights, scandals, even duels—and with major struggles like that of States Rights (with Webster, Calhoun and Clay in the leading roles)—Mrs. Hale ignored all of this. And, by doing so, here once more she made a pattern that women's magazines still follow: a policy of deliberately ignoring matters of fundamental political and economic importance. We do not know whether she did this because she herself was not interested, or because she thought her readers did not know enough to understand them.

This same policy of ignoring matters of fundamental importance is maintained by the women's magazine editors today. Whether they do not know any better themselves, or whether they merely condescend to their readers—in other words holding on to circulation—out of fear that their readers may not be interested in matters that require serious thinking, I am not certain. Possibly both are involved; for truth, like specks of citron in a cake, peeps out from many places.

Although the coming of the Civil War was blackening the sky, Mrs. Hale said little about it. Instead, in 1850, when *Godey's Lady's Book* had a circulation of 150,000, fabulous for that period, she introduced the word *lingerie* to her readers. She explained the meaning of the word and said that it was important for women to have fine white hand-made underthings. It may surprise the woman of today to hear that she met considerable resistance, for some of her readers said, "A waste. Why spend money on what nobody is going to see?"

In 1852 she wrote editorials on "Absent Friends," "A Gossip About Gloves," "A Love Waif," and other such topics, setting the tone and pattern for what women were to read for the coming decades. She regularly ran the departments that today still make up the backbone of the women's magazines: beauty, cooking, health, household decoration, manners, gardening—all the technical information that women needed in their daily work of running a household.

Vernon Parrington, the historian, called *Godey's Lady's Book* "cambric tea." It may have seemed like that to men; it was meant to. But it carried a powerful punch.

James Playsted Wood,[8] said that Mrs. Hale through *Godey's Lady's Book,* affected the manners, morals, tastes, fashions in

[8] James Playsted Wood, *Magazines in the United States,* The Ronald Press, 1949.

clothes, homes and diets of generations of American readers. The magazine did much to form the American woman's ideas of what they were like, how they should act, and how they should insist on being treated.

"It was her taste and her ideas of what was or was not proper material to be spread before the eyes of American womanhood that determined the magazine's contents. A strong editor, she (Sarah Hale) made her magazine a distinct force in American life, just as she and Godey made it a remarkable publishing success. Mrs. Hale campaigned for the recognition of women writers. Before her time, women had either used masculine pseudonyms or initials or had hidden coyly behind anonymity. She had them boldly sign their names. She insisted on the simple and familiar fiction, as against the foreign and extravagant. She introduced Harriet Beecher Stowe, who was still an unknown writer."

Sarah Hale grew old. She gave up her work on the magazine in 1877 and died two years later. Antoine Godey died in 1878. The magazine had begun to fade under the impact of the social changes that resulted from the Civil War. But with the impetus of being an established institution, it lingered on until 1898. Indeed, its influence lingers on, visible within every woman's magazine published since. In the magazines of today, Sarah Josepha Hale would have approved their indirect speech, their flattery, their "do's" and "don't's." But she would have raised her lady-like hand in horror at the muddled sensationalism and sex that she would see today in her printed progeny. Somewhere along the line, her devotion to the ladylike, to achieving for housekeeping the dignity of a profession, and to the holy cause of women's intellectual progress, went awry.

What Are Patterns for?

The poet Amy Lowell wrote
"Christ, what are patterns for?"
The answer's here to Amy's quote—
And many items more. (Corinna Marsh)

On a day in 1863, in what was then the small village of Fitchburg
in Massachusetts, Ellen Butterick was standing at her kitchen
table trying to cut out a shirt for her husband. She had ripped out
an old one to guide her. Thinking of the clothes she was called on
to make, particularly the many required by her children, she
stopped and pointed her great shears at Mr. Butterick. Then, as
casually as one might say "The sun is coming out after a storm,"
the lady made this history-making remark to her husband. "Mr.
Butterick, it would be easier for us to make our children's clothes if
we had a pattern."

She did not dream that she was starting a revolution in women's
clothes, nor that she was taking a great step in democracy and
power for women.

The first step in that revolution had come when Elias Howe

invented the sewing machine in 1841-46. W. E. Woodward, my late husband, said of this: [1]

The invention of the sewing machine by Elias Howe was the most important invention of the nineteenth century from the standpoint of social progress; also it was one of the most ingenious inventions. Its great importance comes from the fact that it liberated women from drudgery of sewing by hand. I think the women of the world ought to put up a monument to Elias Howe as tall as the Statue of Liberty.

Howe was a New England mechanic and after many ups and downs he made a machine that would sew. Before his time many others had tackled the problem, but most of them went the wrong way about it. They tried to imitate, by mechanism, the motions of a woman in the act of sewing—that is passing the needle through the cloth, then turning the needle around and bringing it back the other way.

Howe didn't try to imitate a seamstress. His conception of the matter was original; he approached the problem in a new way. He put the eye of the needle close to its point instead of at the other end. Then he invented a shuttle, or lockstitch device, to catch the thread after it had passed through the cloth. The sewing machine is a most ingenious piece of mechanism.

There is something that gently hints at meekness in the picture of a woman, sitting with a pile of fine white cloth in her lap, her needle sewing a fine seam. And it took time for a woman to do her family's sewing. Indeed her every leisure moment had to be spent that way. Sewing a fine seam took time. A good deal of dressmaking was done by farmwomen during the winter. Most of it was pretty crude. So the invention of the sewing machine gave the woman time. She used the time for a little diversion, maybe,

[1] *The Way Our People Lived* by W. E. Woodward, E. P. Dutton.

but more, she used it for education and for power, although these results did not show at once.

The trend toward democracy took even longer to show up. The machine simplified a woman's work, but it took another big step, one generally ignored by historians, to make her look as fashionable as the aristocrat and, therefore, nearer to social equality. That something started when Mrs. Butterick said it would be a good idea to have patterns for her children's clothes. Patterns for clothes were not new; they had been used for centuries. But like the whole process of securing fashionable clothes, they had been very expensive.

Until the time of the Buttericks, fashion had existed only for the very rich. The middleclass woman, the farmer's wife, had nothing to do with fashion. And the worker's wife was lucky to have one new dress for her wedding.

Martha Washington, for instance, following a fashion mentioned earlier, deposited a mold of her figure with a pattern-maker in London. When she wanted a new gown, she ordered a pattern cut from the mold, either in the actual fabric she had selected or in a cheap cloth. This pattern was then shipped to America and the seamstress made the final garment. At the time of the American Revolution, London was a fashion center and so too was Paris. A mantua-maker would cut the pattern for a wrap or cloak. The word "coat" was used for men's wraps, "mantua" for women's. One mold of the figure lasted for many years since few then dreamed of dieting to reduce. Later the stodgy social life of Queen Victoria and her court and the clothes that went with them robbed London of her place as fashion leader.

For the well-to-do there were also drawings and paper dolls to illustrate the new styles. As in *Godey's Lady's Book,* they were often beautifully done and colored by hand. Among the very rich there was a more appealing method—the use of dolls. Each doll was dressed carefully in the latest fashion. Incidentally, it seems the word "style" was never applied to clothes. "Fashion" was the word. Style was applied to furniture.

It was Queen Isabella of France who started this pretty doll custom. France was already the leader of fashion, when in 1391 Queen Isabella sent a doll to the Queen of England to give her the most up-to-date fashion news from the French capital. It was a graceful and expensive gift and became a model for those who could afford it. Probably much later, some of these dolls were made the full size of a woman.

They called these dolls "babies" or sometimes, "fashion babies," or "little ladies." Wealthy women in our own Colonies had fashionably dressed dolls sent from London.

Alice Morse Earle quotes an advertisement from the *New England Journal,* July 2, 1733:

> To be seen at Mrs. Hannah Teatt's Mantua-maker, at the head of Summer Street, Boston a Baby drest after the newest fashion of mantuas and nightgowns and everything belonging to a Dress. Lattily arrived on *Captain White* from London. Any ladies that desire to see it may either come or send. She will be ready to wait on 'em; if they come to the house. It is Two Shilling & if she waits on 'em it is Seven Shilling.

The dolls were also used to show children's clothes and even baby's clothes. But then the picture changed. I have a photograph of my aunt, taken in 1883. She was certainly a working woman with no money to spare, yet she was wearing an elegant, graceful, form-fitting gown, severe, and demanding a perfect figure. It was made, I remember, from a paper pattern; she owed it to that little family chat between the Buttericks in 1863. Ebenezer approved his wife's notion, but he thought first of men's shirts. These were, of course, made at home, and it was a heavy chore for the women of the family. A man's shirt needed a lot of sewing and wore out fast

even in the solid fabrics of that day. Anyway, in June of 1863, just
before the time of the twin Northern victories of Gettysburg and
Vicksburg, Mr. Butterick made his first paper pattern. But it was
for a man's shirt, not a child's dress.

In Troy, years before, Mrs. Montague had made a man's shirt
with a separate collar for the first time. (If I were an essayist, I
would now wander away from my subject and do an elegant piece
about men's shirts and how their pure white piles of fresh-smelling
crispness are tied up with a certain male dignity that to me has
faded with the figured flashy sports shirt.)

Mr. Butterick hadn't a glimmer of an idea that his shirt pattern
was to start him on the road to fortune, and he would have been
shocked to hear that he was taking a stride toward insuring power
and democracy for women. The second pattern—for a small boy's
suit—was Mr. Butterick's compromise with his wife. Mrs. Butterick, it is said, then kept on laying out patterns for ladies' clothes.

The Buttericks immediately began to put their patterns on tissue
paper. These were folded and instructions were pinned on the outside. Later the tissues were enclosed in an envelope with a drawing and instructions on the outside of the envelope. (It seems remarkable that until recently it did not occur to the pattern makers
to print instructions on each individual piece of paper.) Apparently
this happened in one of the nicks of history's time, because within
one year the business outgrew little Fitchburg, and in 1864 Mr.
Butterick opened an office on Broadway in New York. The patterns grew in variety until some sort of catalogue was necessary.

Thus, quite naturally, out of a real need, a magazine came into
existence. First called the *Metropolitan Monthly;* in 1875 it became
the *Delineator.* It was sold for fifteen cents a copy. After 1900, the
Butterick Company added another magazine, the *Designer.* This
was sold for ten cents a copy and carried a cheaper grade of pattern.

Four years later *Harper's Bazaar* was established and sold patterns for twenty-five cents each. Its styles originated from Paris. They were followed by a number of magazines; some conducted their pattern business as a side issue, some were supported by their pattern business.

At first all the patterns were sold by mail; but by 1869 they were distributed through department stores, and soon the Butterick Company established branch offices and agencies. By 1871 they were selling six million patterns a year. Each pattern was used by its owner and many of her friends. Even now the pattern business runs into the millions, and with the increase of sales of sewing machines, it keeps on growing. The Butterick Company, while large, today has only a fraction of the pattern business. There are a number of large pattern companies, some owned by magazines, some independent. They are sold through five-and-ten-cent stores, department stores, supermarkets, etc.

There were real, even sharp distinctions between classes in this country. The women of the upper classes were distinguished on sight by their clothes from the middle or lower classes. The words "lower classes" were accepted as meaning people with small incomes.

The wealthy could get their fashion news in many ways, by letters, by dolls, by individual patterns cut in London and Paris. A poorer woman wore clothes which suited her, but were not in the first fashion. Now the effect of clothes upon manners is well known; for instance a woman dressed up at a masquerade ball as a queen, adopts a stately manner. So as soon as a woman in a plain workaday dress met another in the newest frills and doodads of fashion, the former was likely to accept a second place in life.

The coming of cheap paper patterns eroded that situation. A skilled seamstress could work from the paper pattern, because such a pattern, while a simplification of the fancy styles, had the same lines. The average woman for the first time could realize how much more important they were than trimmings, bows and bangles, to which she had resorted before she had a pattern.

This was how fashion reached the multitudes and how the wide difference between classes, as indicated by women's and children's clothes, began to disappear in this country.

However, the designs in the early catalogues show nothing of this tendency. If anything, they were more elaborate than those of Civil War days, and, even with the sewing machine, involved an immense amount of hand work. But gradually, in order to increase sales, the patterns were made simpler in design. Of course the kind of work women were beginning to do in offices and factories had some influence in this simplification. Yet when these fussy patterns came out most women were working very hard in their own kitchens.

To look at these pictures of the 1870 designs one would not dream that any woman ever lifted her delicate hands to handle a broom or a dishpan. The only indication that a woman ever did any work about the house was the multiplicity of her aprons. Aprons! Aprons! Old-fashioned women made it a matter of pride that they could wash a great pan of dirty dishes without getting a drop on an apron. The apron patterns were often fancy and part of dressing up for company.

Aprons, aprons, plain, big, small, ruffled, made of silk or cotton or black alpaca cross-stitched. The importance of the apron is indicated by its price. It cost as much as the pattern of a basque, fifteen cents or sixpence. (All prices are given in the catalogue in the English coinage as well as American. Perhaps because the Butterick Company did business in England.) Fifteen cents was the average price of a pattern.

The dress-up apron came back into fashion later, but not with the same mien. Then it was for "company," now it is for "guests." There's a difference—a drop in humanity and warmth between the words. But except for the apron, there is no hint in the clothes or the fashion notes of that day that women had to do any work at home. I can remember, as a child, a couple of decades later, how women at their housework wore long wide ample aprons of checked blue-and-white gingham. They were tied with a bow in the back, and for company there were equally ample starched aprons of snowy white. In my memory these stand for stability, kindness and generous hospitality. Can this be equally true of a child whose mother wears slacks or shorts? Maybe!

Early refusal to recognize that women were doing a lot of work for which their ruffles and trains were a nuisance is the more amazing when we remember what that housework involved. For instance, the *Delineator* of January, 1886, suggests that the reader take a walk before breakfast and then cook up the following menus for an average day. On a coal or wood stove, of course.

BREAKFAST
Cooked Wheat with Cream
A Ragout, or Mutton Chop
Lyonnaise Potatoes   Graham Gems
White and Graham Breads
Coffee

(She didn't buy bread, she baked it.)

LUNCHEON OR SUPPER
Biscuit
Warm Meat in Slices
Baked or Fried Potatoes   Canned or Cooked Fruit
Rebecca Cake
Tea or Chocolate

(A can actually! But no electric mixer. Not even a potato parer!)

DINNER
Tomato or Bisque Soup
Baked Fish, with Oyster Sauce
Roast Goose

Apple Sauce   Boiled Onions
Potato Puff   Celery Salad

Spanish Cream

Nuts   Fruit

Coffee

(She didn't catch the fish but that's about all she didn't do.)

To wash the dishes for all these meals—consider what it meant! First, on your wood or coal stove you heated a great kettle of water. Then you poured it into a big dishpan, made suds with homemade or Babbitt's soap. You washed the glasses, rubbed the forks and knives with a scraping of Sapolio, which was the only real help at the time, washed the greasy plates with a dishrag, emptied the basin, filled it again, rinsed everything in clean hot water, washed out the dishrag, washed the dishpan, dried the dishes, polished the silver, washed the dish towels.

A Sapolio advertisement of the time that shows squalling children pulling at a mother's dress, with its long sleeves, high neck, and small waist, reads:

> Oh my, was ever such a go!
> They all want hand Sapolio.
> Be quiet do, for mercy's sake
> And I will bring you each a cake.

The patterns of the seventies and eighties treated all women as delicate ladies to the point of *grotesquerie*. Their pictures showed these creatures in paper-soled shoes even if they were knee-deep in snowdrifts. Particularly impractical were the ruffles at the end of the sleeves at the wrists. Imagine scrambling eggs wearing these! For daytime use there were no short sleeves at all. Actually, at housework the women simply rolled up their sleeves. Now and then there were some signs of sanity in clothes. For instance there were nurse's caps for "practical" nurses, there were waterproof hoods—so we know that at least some women did go out in the rain—and dust-caps—to tell us that the dainty ladies did do some housework.

Also—and this I envy them—there were patterns for chatelaines. A chatelaine was a capacious pocket sewed to a belt or hanging on a string, in which to carry a handkerchief, keys, pencil, or what you needed as you went about your work.

For "misses and girls," the designs were the same as for their mothers, only smaller, the costume consisting of basque, walking skirt, overskirt and sack, all worn at the same time. The overskirt was elaborate and could be put on over the utility skirt. For "tiny girls," three to nine years, the same as above.

Then for the "infants," long dresses, wrapper robes, slips, cloaks, including double circular caped cloaks, bibs, sacks. Also for the poor infant, shirts, drawers, pinning blankets, etc., etc. Doll clothes were the only light touch, but even the dolls were as elaborately caparisoned as the adult lady.

And for boys there were cadet suits, yachting costumes with big sailor-collars, kilt costumes, Hussar jackets. The children sometimes became quite reckless, they played croquet or rolled hoops or sat by the side of streams. They wore hats, of course, and high button shoes. The lowest grade in human society was the barefoot child. Those little dolled-up boys—how did they ever grow up to be the strong tough men of that era? [2]

[2] The Butterick Company says that about the year 1900 two small boys of the British Royal Family wore sailor suits made from Butterick patterns. One of the small boys became George V, King of England; the other became Edward, Duke of Windsor.

The house was as wrapped up and trimmed and suffocated as the person. The catalogue contains patterns for lambrequins, tied back with rich tassels . . . price fifteen cents or sixpence sterling. Everything was rewrapped when possible and embroidered, like the "Ladies' nightdress case," embroidered with the words, "Good Night," ten cents. Taste, as one can see, was appalling.

The small waist was the sexual implication in fashionable clothes. It was a particularly prim period. Even then, doctors protested against it as a health danger. Later the bustle came in. It was surely as crude a symbol as any that ever appeared in women's clothes.

No matter how prim the period, the sex symbol has always appeared. The crinolines of the sixties got their start in the Empress Eugénie's pregnancy, and later the bust line was accentuated and exposed. Back in medieval times a protruding belly padded to look larger than possible was the fashion. This was at a time when men preferred pregnant women, as some say they do today in parts of southern Italy, for example. But in the fifteenth and sixteenth centuries men responded by wearing a codpiece.

Any part of a woman's body can be enticing or erotic, depending upon where and when. In Bali before the Second World War, the breasts were considered the sex symbol; so when the Dutch ordered the Balinese women to cover their breasts on meeting a white man, they quite innocently did so by throwing their skirts up over their heads. This was considered all right.

With the growth of democracy for men in the early nineteenth century, their clothes grew more severe, and they abandoned the silks and satins of earlier centuries. As I look today at men's gay sports clothes and blue dinner jackets and nylon shirts I wonder if men are again seeking to shine by seeming, rather than by doing, and maybe women, simplifying their dress, are seeking to shine by doing rather than by being.

It is almost as though in these clothes there was a last-stand fight going on against the real advance of both democracy and power for women. The very names given to the gowns of the eighties denote elegance and snobbery, names like "Ladies' Princess Polonaise," or "Duchesses' Waists For Evening." In a catalogue of 1876 the beautiful engravings show "ladies of refined taste" sitting on elegant Victorian chairs, with fringed footstools, at tea tables, looking at portfolios. Here and there one clad in a "Princess Polonaise" holds a beruffled baby. This was before the pattern makers realized that it was not as easy to show the lines of a gown when a woman was sitting down. These drawings also showed the whole figure in the proportion of six times the length of the head, which are the actual proportions of the body. Later fashion publicity got impossible grace by drawing all figures eight times the length of the head. In that way the picture showed a figure that was long and slim. This has been more or less abandoned now, replaced by photographs. The tall, bony, extra-thin model of today represents this same abnormality.

Weight reduction was not a serious problem among these ladies. The sizes given for ladies' clothes were, on the average, larger than they are today. A lady's close-fitting basque came in sizes 28 to 46 inch bust. Waist measurements began at 20 and ran up to 36 inches. The twenty-inch waist was then the sex attraction; the thirty-six-inch waist was accepted as normal for middle-aged women.

There was no concession, direct or oblique, to the growing suffrage movement or to the few women who worked in mills and, here and there, in telegraph offices. But then women had one right that they lost and now at last have regained. The ads at that time showed a woman who is obviously a lady, well bred and well dressed, and she is offering her guests a tray with a carafe of whiskey and glasses. Women lost the right to serve liquor—at least in advertisements—as the years went by. But I see that they are recovering this right. After Prohibition disappeared, the liquor industry decided that if they showed women in their ads in any way, even looking on while men of distinction raptly regarded their drinks, Prohibition would come back. So, women were banished from the company of men of distinction. But, according to the *New York Times* of February 2, 1959, "Score another for the women. In a couple of weeks, Lord Calvert will introduce a 'Lady of Distinction.' "

Next, women will probably be allowed to hold a liquor glass and then—who knows—take a sip. This is a reasonable enough expectation when you compare it with the advertising of cigarettes. For decades women were not allowed actually to smoke a cigarette in any advertisement. This taboo gave way a little in the thirties when they were shown in one advertisement with the caption, "Blow a puff my way." And now look at the thing! In a current television ad, a girl is shown smoking two cigarettes at once!

5 ∬

The *Delineator*

In 1868 Ebenezer Butterick started his magazine, the *Metropolitan Monthly*. It had grown out of the pattern business. In 1875 the *Delineator* replaced *Metropolitan Monthly*. Of course, it did not call itself just a pattern magazine; it was "A Journal of Fashion, Culture and Fine Arts." That was partly justified by its price of fifteen cents at a time when most magazines were still only ten cents.

In attitude it was not much different from *Godey's Lady's Book,* but that magazine had declined in quality and standing. The *Delineator* put a great deal of emphasis on etiquette and on behavior, some of which, surprisingly enough, seemed rather modern. For instance, it scolded its readers for looking into shop windows and using them as mirrors while they powdered their faces. Incidentally, scolding the reader has always been a common practice with women's magazines.

A series of women's magazines followed: *McCall's* in 1870, *Woman's Home Companion* in 1873, *Ladies' Home Journal* in 1883, *Good Housekeeping* in 1885. All these magazines were fairly similar in contents and point of view. There was no major change among them until Edward Bok took over the *Ladies' Home Journal* in 1889.

Meantime, the *Delineator* (and what we say of it applies to the others, too) got its circulation through agents or by mail. Evidently there was a great deal of impersonation by people who pretended to be agents and kept the money. This advertisement and others like it appeared frequently:

Caught and Imprisoned!

(A list of names of 16 men followed)

The above is a list of the parties who have been tried, convicted and sentenced to imprisonment for obtaining money under false pretenses by representing themselves as Agents for this Company, and taking subscriptions to our publication or establishing fictitious agencies for the sale of our patterns. In each of these cases we have paid a reward of $100 to the party or parties entitled to the same.

(The advertisement then offered to continue the reward for similar captures.)

Our Authorized Representatives—(able at all times to produce abundant evidence of his authority to act for us) . . . Our traveling agents are gentlemen (we have no lady travelers). . . .

We especially warn the public against the following pretended canvassing agents: (names of about 40 men, 1 woman, and the states they traveled in).

Often the magazine gave a subscription free with some other purchase, but that method, used by nearly all the magazines in earlier times, was stopped by the Post Office between 1908 and 1912. After that any magazine offered free lost its special mailing rate. The magazines thereupon asked payment for the magazine and gave away with it a book or premium. Same idea, different words.

One department of the *Delineator* was called the Children's Corner. For about fifty years most of the women's magazines had special departments directed to children. These have long been abandoned, but in the *Delineator* of January, 1886, the following appeared:

In this department devoted to dolls' furniture last month, we gave our young friends a treat, and at the same time promised they should have another this month. It is not hard to picture to ourselves the pleased and happy faces of the little innocents as their eyes meet the different pieces shown this month for their special benefit, and with the knowledge of their pleasure we shall feel amply repaid. This month, the little ones have a "corner" devoted to themselves, and a cosy little corner it will be, full of bright, industrious, funloving little people, all anxious to do their very best in their make-believe carpentering work. During the long days to be spent indoors, the amusement afforded in this corner will, we trust, bring much pleasure to the little ones, and keep them from mischief—for a while at least.

Directions for cutting out pasteboard or Bristol Board, the pieces to be covered with plain satin or silk or some pretty chintz, flowered sateen-topped goods, fancy paper, gilt or silver paper or any nice fabric.

There were few advertisements in the early magazines for women. The mechanism for handling advertising was quite different from what it is today. Now it is customary for an advertiser to appoint an agency which handles its publicity and sometimes its merchandising. At the time covered here, an individual or a company bought all the advertising space in a magazine and then re-sold it to separate advertisers.

Standards were low in all these magazines. There was plenty of questionable patent medicine advertising. Here is a sample:

"Sent PREPAID ON TRIAL." This ad contained seventeen

letters purporting to be sent by satisfied users, "who suffered from
muscular rheumatism, back trouble, kidney, liver and nervous
trouble, back and spinal trouble, indigestion, acute dyspepsia"—
all of which were cured by Dr. Scott's Genuine Miracle.

There were also Obesity Fruit Salts, no doubt a violent cathartic.

The soap ads were much more wholesome. There were Ivory
Soap, Pears' Soap, Packer's Tar Soap (and, by the way, what
ever happened to Fairy Soap?). In January, 1886, Ivory Soap sang
this song:

> John Anderson, my Jo, John,
>   When first I was your wife,
> On every washing day, John,
>   I wearied my life.
> It made you cross to see, John,
>   Your shirts not white as snow,
> I washed them with our home-made soap,
>   John Anderson, my Jo.
> Ah! Many a quarrel then, John,
>   Had you and I together,
> But now all that is changed, John,
>   We'll never have another:
> For washed with Ivory Soap, John,
>   Your shirts are white as snow,
> And now I smile on washing day,
>   John Anderson, my Jo.

Ivory Soap advertisements ran often. They were set up to look
as nearly as possible like editorial matter. One showed a charming
sketch of a woman at a washboard, another one showed her hanging clothes on the line. Both women were wearing tight basques
and overskirts. They were very elegant, except that their sleeves
were rolled to the elbow. In none of these was the word "Ivory"
or the Proctor and Gamble name displayed. There was just a cake
of soap on the washboard, vaguely identified as Ivory.

Another advertisement really showed some progress among women:

> OVER 125 Girls
> Have now been educated
> In music, Art, Elocution, Sculpture, Etc.
> Under the Plan of
> THE LADIES' HOME JOURNAL

These girls tell themselves, how they did it in a little book, which will be sent free to any address by
THE CURTIS PUBLISHING COMPANY, PHILADELPHIA

An important part of the magazine was the answering of questions. Some of these:

To acknowledge an invitation from a gentleman.

How to use large bronze buttons.

Where books on Palmistry may be obtained.

How a brown brocaded plush wrap might be trimmed.

The fact that there is no need to thank the one who has played a game of croquet with you.

That a person in deep mourning should not make ceremonious visits until the expiration of a year.

For mourning: "If you did not wear a veil when first you went into mourning, it would be in extremely bad taste to assume one later."

There was a little attention to exercise. There was a foolish something called Delsarte. Delsarte was a Frenchman who invented a system of calisthenics by means of gestures. He divided the body into three parts, the head (intellectual), the trunk (emotional), the limbs (physical). It was the rage from the 1850's to the 1890's and was one of the silliest exhibits of the century. The lessons as they appeared in the *Delineator* received the hearty approval of the most prominent educators in the country. Even Webster defined Delsarte as a system of calisthenics; it remained fashionable until 1900.

We all know that everything was much cheaper at that time than now, but we cannot resist quoting a few items as they were advertised in the *Delineator:*

> Sealskin cloaks—$185
> Shoes, patent-leather trimmed—59c
> Kid gloves—59c
> Hosiery—35c
> Sewing Machine from Sears Roebuck—$12.50

By 1894 there were signs of education. An article in the *Delineator* on Wellesley College, for instance, contained the following:

For board and lodging in the excellently arranged rooms within the college bldgs., the charge is only $200 a year. Each girl is still expected to do a very small amount of work in the care of the various buildings, but each year narrows the range of these duties.

RELAXATION—If, however, the college atmosphere grows monotonous, and the students long to see men and women from the outer world, they may serve tea to their friends on Saturday afternoon and evening or on Monday afternoon in the parlors of the various buildings.

And showing that women did work outside the home there was an article on jobs in telegraphy as employment for women. Both these articles were in the July issue of the *Delineator* in 1894.

Butterick started another magazine. The *Designer,* which was sold at ten cents a copy, was thinner and of a slightly lower grade than the *Delineator*. It sold cheaper patterns of simpler syles than the parent magazine.

In its later years, the *Delineator* went through some curious didos. In the early 1900's Theodore Dreiser, the great American novelist, became its editor. He was out of place, since he was no executive, and since he understood only one kind of woman, the kind called at that time, "a lady of easy virtue." But out of his experience, he found one of his novels, *The Genius*. While he was there, the *Delineator* had signed a contract with a man named Ralph Tilton to sell advertising. Tilton was "The Genius." He had a fabulous and deserved reputation as a brilliant copy-writer. In the gigantic advertising world of today, no one stands out. But in the 1890's and 1900's, the business was smaller, people in it knew each other better, and there was more room for originality. The only evidence that remains of Tilton's originality is the coupon. The coupon is such a commonplace of pressure-selling today, that it seems incredible that once upon a time there was no coupon.

I saw him once, a dark, handsome man, with a romantic halo. His mother had been involved in a famous scandal, and his father had sued her for divorce, naming Henry Ward Beecher as co-respondent. I am sure that Tilton himself did not consider this connection romantic. Indeed it probably ruined his life. At any rate, he died at thirty-seven, and when he died his wife faced the world without money. A woman not his wife tried to kill herself, while another woman merely fainted.

But he was at the top of his form when he signed the contract with Butterick for $30,000 a year—a huge salary for that period. His methods and extravagance drove the magazine owners to desperation. There was an account in Chicago he was trying to get; at the outside it might have spent $40,000 a year in the magazine. To get this business, he chartered a New York Central train, filled it with champagne and girls and friends and set off for Chicago. It was no use to call him down or try to put reins on him. Instead the publishers played a trick on him. They raised his pay. He celebrated that raise. The raise broke his contract and he was out of a job.

However, the *Delineator* shook off all that nonsense and once more became a sober-sided magazine of standard size and character until 1937 when the Butterick Company realized that the general magazine business was not worth its while. It quietly folded both magazines and went entirely into the pattern business, which made real money.

I have chosen the Butterick Company to tell some of the story of the paper pattern because it was the first in the field. But there are many others, and many just as successful. But chiefly I am trying to show that these cheap and easy-to-follow paper patterns have had an incalculable influence in pushing forward equality among women. The patterns naturally made their clothes more alike, greatly decreased the sharp difference between the clothes of women of different social circles. Paper patterns also gave them more leisure and that increased their power. All this has been much further advanced by the manufacture of good women's clothes at low prices.

6

The *Ladies' Home Journal*
Gets a Father

If Sarah Josepha Hale was the mother of American women's magazines, Edward Bok was their father. Though methods and manners are different today, these two still dominate the women's magazine family.

In 1879 Cyrus K. Curtis was publishing a four-page weekly called the *Tribune and Farmer,* for which he charged fifty cents a year. He thought it would be a good idea to run a column to be called "Women and the Home" in this sheet, but he had no conception of the difference between a woman's mind and a man's. He would merely clip items from other periodicals and bring them home and try them out on his wife.

"Who gets up this column?" she asked one evening.

"I do," he said.

"If you really knew how funny all this sounds to a woman, you would laugh." [1]

Mrs. Curtis took over the department and by 1883, it became so popular that Cyrus and his wife decided to make it a separate

[1] From *A Man From Maine* by Edward Bok.

magazine, which they called the *Ladies' Journal*. Through a printing error the word "Home" appeared in the title and they left it that way. It was an accident, but it reflected a change of attitude on what a woman's magazine could mean in the life of a household, an attitude that Edward Bok later turned into something like a campaign with battles that were gentle but firm.

Within five years, the combined magazines had 48,000 subscriptions. Thereupon Mr. Curtis sold the *Tribune and Farmer* and really got to work on the *Ladies' Home Journal*. By artful advertising and reduced rate subscription offers, he raised the circulation to 100,000 copies. He decided then to get better writers, like Marion Harland, a leading authority on housekeeping. A novelist. She hesitated at first, but when Curtis offered her ninety dollars for a story, she couldn't resist. Mrs. Curtis was horrified.

"How many stories do we get for ninety dollars?" she demanded.

"One," her husband replied.

"One! Do you want to bankrupt us!" [2]

But Mr. Curtis managed to sell ninety dollars worth of advertising space to an egg-beater manufacturer who admired Marion Harland's writing. So it all worked out fine, and the Curtises felt free to approach other popular writers like Louisa M. Alcott. The magazine circulation jumped to 700,000 copies and Curtis took the reckless step of raising the price to a dollar a year, whereupon his printer remarked, "Curtis's success has gone to his head."

And, indeed, circulation did fall off at first. At the same time, Mrs. Curtis resigned as editor. Edward Bok, who was working at Scribner's, stepped in, and from this moment the *Ladies' Home Journal* began to develop into an American institution. Bok took over the editing of the magazine in 1889, when it was six years old. Cyrus K. Curtis had edited it largely by guess; it had little

[2] From *A Man From Maine* by Edward Bok.

that was fresh in content. Bok brought to it an over-all plan, an organization of the material and a purpose.

In 1889 *Godey's Lady's Book* was fading. For Mrs. Hale and Antoine Godey, the female of the species had been a lady; for Edward Bok she was a woman. Sarah Josepha Hale had built iron fences to protect her sex from its own weakness. Bok began, methodically and with determination, to break these fences down. The lady was still an ideal, but Bok had a deeper conception, and slowly but steadily the idea of *lady* gave way to his idea of a *woman*.

To be sure, the public was ready for the change of attitude. The spread of feminine democracy and of work outside the home had made the *lady* old-fashioned, even foolish. Just what was meant by *woman* as opposed to *lady* becomes clear when we realize what made Bok think the way he did. His mother and grandmother were Dutch, strong, able women of lower middle-class stock with no fancy notions. They were self-disciplined, with high ideals, but practical, ambitious and careful about money. Bok adored them both. More important, he respected them. That respect he showed in the editing of the *Ladies' Home Journal*.

He was also a very ambitious man who made almost a religion of getting ahead; he believed that, like himself, everyone should try to "lift" himself in the world. That applied as well to "herself." In his mind "lifting" meant better physical or material conditions, better taste, more money, and being as good as your neighbors. As it turned out, *seeming* as good as your neighbors took the place of *being* as good. A few years later, Hearst's *New York Journal* began a cartoon series called "Keeping Up With The Joneses." That was what the *Ladies' Home Journal* meant, and partly what Bok meant, but he would have resented such an expression of it as vulgar.

Mr. Bok was unquestionably a brilliant, original and daring man. In 1921 he wrote an autobiography which he called *The*

Americanization of Edward Bok. It is probable that this book—
quite contrary to the author's intention—turned many young
people into social rebels.

When Bok was a little boy, he had an amazing talent for seeing
a penny around any corner, and he tells with pride how he
acquired a good many pennies. In the open streetcars of the period,
people often seemed to get very thirsty. Little Edward would
appear with a bucket of water and sell it at a penny a cup. When
this business grew too big, he hired other little boys and divided
with them, three pennies for himself and one for the other boy.
It is not clear why these other children did not go into business on
their own, but even as a boy, Bok was an executive of high power.
At the same time, Edward was collecting some remarkable friends
among famous people.

This is how he did it: He was a poor boy and had to leave school
early. He set out to educate himself, and he did this with determination and with some original ideas, too. He began by collecting postage stamps. He said that helped him with geography. It
also gave him the idea that "autograph letters from famous persons
would be of equal service in his struggle for self-education." (Bok
always wrote of himself in the third person.)

Then, as he says, "with boyish frankness" he wrote a letter on
"some mooted question" to some famous people. They were kind
to him. He showed a valuable talent for getting along with prominent people.

Bok must have had a good deal of charm. The following from
The Americanization of Edward Bok, is one example:

He noticed that these New England authors rarely visited New York,
or if they did, their presence was not heralded by the newspapers among
the "distinguished arrivals." He had a great desire to meet these writers;
and having saved a little money he decided to take his week's summer
vacation in the winter, when he knew he should be more likely to find

the people of his quest at home, and to spend his savings on a trip to Boston. He had never been away from home, so this trip was a momentous affair.

He arrived in Boston on Sunday evening; and the first thing he did was to dispatch a note, by messenger, to Doctor Oliver Wendell Holmes, announcing the important fact that he was there, and what his errand was, and asking whether he might come up and see Doctor Holmes any time the next day. Edward naively told him that he could come as early as Doctor Holmes liked—by breakfast time, he was assured, as Edward was all alone!

Doctor Holmes' amusement at this ingenuous note may be imagined. Within the hour, the messenger brought back this answer:

My dear Boy:

I shall certainly look for you tomorrow morning at eight o'clock to have a piece of pie with me. That is real New England, you know.

> Very cordially yours,
> Oliver Wendell Holmes.

Edward was there at eight o'clock. Strictly speaking, he was there at seven-thirty, and found the author already at his desk in that room, overlooking the Charles River.

"Well," was the cheery greeting, "you couldn't wait until eight for your breakfast, could you? Neither could I when I was a boy. I used to have my breakfast at seven." And then telling the boy all about his boyhood, the cheery poet led him to the dining room, and for the first time he breakfasted away from home and ate pie—and that with "The Autocrat" at his own breakfast table!

A cosier time no boy could have had. Just the two were there, and the smiling face that looked out over the plates and cups gave the boy courage to tell all that this trip was going to mean to him.

"And you have come on just to see us, have you?" chuckled the poet. "Now tell me, what good do you think you will get out of it?"

He was told that the idea was; that every successful man had something to tell a boy that would be likely to help him, and that Edward wanted to see the men who had written the books that people enjoyed. Doctor Holmes could not conceal his amusement at all this.

Later Bok had lunch with Longfellow, who told him he liked *Evangeline* better than *Hiawatha,* and asked him to say grace in Dutch. And then Longfellow had him to supper and the theater.

His biggest hit was with Ulysses S. Grant, the President of the United States. He wrote a letter asking the President some question, and this started Bok on a lifelong friendship with Grant and his wife. Both in money and influence, this "frank, youthful and direct" campaign rolled up a mighty profit for Bok. He made himself a symbol of youth, eager to learn, questioning the learned and important men of that period for their wisdom. Many newspaper stories and sermons held up his enterprise as an example to other boys.

Bok was twenty-six when he took over as editor of the *Ladies' Home Journal.* He was, according to the historian James Playsted Wood, "young, didactic, self-assured." The magazine had a circulation of 700,000. Its price was a dollar a year. Bok's brilliant editing soon made that circulation look like peanuts.

He was the youngest and the highest-paid editor of his time. At first there was a good deal of shock at the idea that a man was to edit a woman's magazine. Many men thought he must be effeminate. Bok and Curtis turned this shock into handsome publicity, because it soon became apparent that Bok had a remarkable understanding of the woman's mind. He had also, at the beginning, some idealistic ideas about women that he got from his grandmother and his mother. This idealism received a good many blows. When, after thrity years as editor, he resigned in 1919, newspaper men asked him what he thought about women. He says in his autobiography that he refused to answer.

In 1889, it was not usual for editors' names to appear on a magazine masthead, nor did they sign their editorials. Bok began to sign his name to what he wrote, and he put his name on the masthead, too. In this there was, no doubt, some vanity, but there was also a sound business reason. By establishing his own responsibility, he was helping his later campaigns. This was a beginning which other editors gladly followed.

Like Sarah Josepha Hale, he hid a steely command under silken words. He said he wanted to give his readers "uplift and inspiration" as well as specific help for women's daily needs. However stuffy the language he used, however stuffy the sentiments he expressed, that's what the readers wanted—millions of them.

Bok quickly showed himself a pioneer. He moved forward on three roads. First, he set out to improve the taste of America. Here he tried hard with supreme self-confidence.

Second, he broadened the contents of his magazine by using more articles of public interest and he had better writers than his predecessors in magazines like *Delineator* ever thought of employing. But he kept closely to the idea that he was putting out a trade paper for women, though he would not have put it so simply.

In his third venture on the magazine, his courage deserves a high salute. This covered his campaign for "causes." Some of them were trivial, but some were on an idealistic level. Frequently, he risked a loss of circulation and of advertising. In such cases, he stuck to his guns, or gave up only when the situation became hopeless. As will be shown later, he fought some of his campaigns to victory to the everlasting benefit of the country. Sarah Josepha Hale had also fought through campaigns for what she thought would be the betterment of women. But her campaigns were for large generalities. Bok stuck to smaller and more precise objectives. And, by doing so, his magazine fitted in better with the minds of his readers.

As to taste, for two generations the *Ladies' Home Journal* has claimed that Bok "improved the taste of the American home." Bok says he was appalled by the architecture of the small house of the period (the eighties and nineties). There were filagrees piled on turrets, machine-made ornaments on windows, doors and roofs, as well as other gingerbread horrors. Most of the houses were put up without the help of architects. Bok wanted desperately to introduce better houses to the American public. He decided it would be a good idea to have a number of architects make plans and show them in his magazine. It seems odd today that most of the architects refused to take part because they thought doing so would "cheapen their profession." Finally he got one architect who was willing to take a risk and together they worked out plans for a house. Architects all over the country were miffed, and calmed down only when they say how much business they got from people who weren't any longer satisfied with home-made plans.

In July 1897, he showed this house in the *Ladies' Home Journal* as a model for a suburban "home." The house had nine rooms, a bath, a large porch. The kitchen was spacious, and all of it could be built in that rich day when dollars bought so much, for from two thousand dollars to twenty-five hundred dollars.

Several hundred people copied it exactly, and if the lingering landscape means anything, thousands more adapted plans from this high-shouldered, frowning-roof structure. Bok says that for twenty-five years the *Ladies' Home Journal* showed these plans, and entire colonies of *Ladies' Home Journal* houses sprang up. Dressed up with shrubs, this model house had a homey, comfortable look, but that look was deceptive. It was really a model of discomfort, bad lighting and close, shrugging lines. Only the wide, long porch and the big kitchen looked open and welcoming.

In another issue, Bok showed the Louis Tiffany house that used to stand at Seventy-ninth Street and Madison Avenue in New York. He called it "the most artistic home" in the city. In Bok's time the word "artistic" had not been downgraded to its present questionable estate. But that Tiffany house! I remember it. When I was a little girl it used to frighten me as I passed by on the way to Central Park. It was dark gray, grim-looking, heavy enough to withstand a siege—a stone-age fortress.

Bok himself so admired the model house he showed in his magazine that he later built an enlarged copy of it for himself. His own house, which he built after he married the daughter of the Curtises, was wider and more open, but it was just as cluttered with decorations and it just as desperately shut out sun and light.

Bok told an amusing story about the approach to his marriage with young Miss Curtis. What a cautious, planning-ahead man he was! He was in Europe with Cyrus Curtis, when Curtis happened to begin talking about his daughter. Bok writes that "certain signals had already passed between the latter and myself. . . . It had never occurred to him (Curtis) that anything save the most casual acquaintance existed between his editor and his daughter."

One day we were riding from Calais to Paris when he said:

"My wife says that daughter is showing evidence of being interested in some young man—she is quiet, very thoughtful and all that. Of course my wife is wrong," he continued with perfect self-sufficiency.

"Daughter is too young for that sort of thing."

This was a line of talk in which I was, of course, intensely interested, and I determined to follow up the advantage.

"That may be, but some day that fact will face you. What then?"

"Oh yes, of course, some day. . . . Well I hope the fellow will be a decent chap; not one of those I see standing on the steps of the hotels sucking cigarettes."

I was smoking a cigarette at that moment, this was not an auspicious beginning.

"What's the matter with an occasional cigarette?" I ventured.

He laughed. "Well," he said, "not as you smoke a cigarette, but you know the type I mean."

"What kind of a chap have you in mind for your daughter?" I ventured.

"I want him to be, first of all, decent. Then I ask that he will be a good business man. He need not have arrived, of course, so long as I can see that he has the qualities for effective work. I intend to have these two things looked into."

"How?" I asked.

"Have his private life looked into by a detective and his business standing by Bradstreet right away," he answered decisively, and the thought seemed to give him infinite satisfaction.

When somewhat later the suitor (Bok, himself) for his daughter's hand came to him, the young man added that he was perfectly willing to be looked up by a detective and Bradstreet!

He looked at the young man, lit a cigar, smiled wanly, and said, "Yes, I suppose so." [3]

It is natural enough, from our present vantage point, to look with condescension on Mr. Bok's taste in houses and to blame him for the atrocities he taught Americans to like. But some of what he proposed was at least better than its immediate predecessors. For the architecture fashionable at the time was ugly. The major harm was not caused by Edward Bok's mistakes in taste, but by the insistence of the *Ladies' Home Journal* for many years afterward that he had "improved the taste of the American home." As for Bok, it is too bad that he had the opportunity to influence American taste and only misdirected it. Bok was familiar with the beautiful interiors of Back Bay houses in Boston, and the lovely brick barns on Pennsylvania farms, and the sweeping curves and

[3] From *A Man From Maine.*

austere beauty of Southern plantation houses. Yet he had preferred the Tiffany house and its progeny.[4]

An effort toward better furnishing of the small American house
followed. Bok was convinced that articles and pictures on furnishings and interior decorations would interest his readers. But he
was baffled as to the best method to go about this, until one day he
met a friend who told him she was on her way to a funeral.

> "I didn't know you were so well acquainted with Mrs. S. . . . ," said Bok.
> "I wasn't, as a matter of fact," replied the woman. "I'll be perfectly
> frank; I am going to the funeral just to see how Mrs. S . . .'s house is
> furnished. She was always thought to have great taste, you know, and
> whether you know it or not, a woman is always keen to look into another
> woman's home." [5]

That gave him the idea of showing photographs of interiors
under the heading "Good Taste and Bad Taste." This has been
done often since, but it was revolutionary at the time.

Bok's houses were really "decorated." Not one inch was let
alone. "Cozy corners" were especially satisfying for this purpose.
The washstand is decorated with ruffled curtains which reveal the
bowl and pitcher, but are half open below, merely hinting genteely
at other articles.

The vogue for furniture was for oak, some good, some bad. The
pity of it was that good old plain mahogany furniture was often
sold for nearly nothing, or removed to the garret and replaced by
yellow oak. Houses badly furnished were perhaps improved by
Bok's suggestions. But others, clean, simple and uncluttered, were
turned into mausoleums. All this was a conscious step in the mind

---

[4] There were exceptions to Edward Bok's bad taste. A farmhouse shown
in the October, 1900, issue was very good.
[5] From *The Americanization of Edward Bok.*

of Edward Bok, as editor of the *Ladies' Home Journal,* toward a policy known later as "Keeping up with the Joneses."

His next step was to try to improve the pictures on the walls of the American home. (He never called it a "house," but always a "home.") Within a year he had decorated American homes with 100,000 copies of such pictures as "The Hanging of the Crane," and "Home-Keeping-Hearts." Perhaps they were an improvement on the stuffy enlargements of photographs of Grandma and Grandpa. But surely they were no better than the hand-cross-stitched "Home-Sweet-Home."

Bok was ready to move outside the home in his march toward better taste, or as he put it in his biography, "contribute to elevate the standard of public taste." He says he was surprised to learn that newly-rich women regarded the Pullman car as a model of taste to be followed in their own parlors. He says that at the turn of the century the "decoration of the Pullman car was atrocious." And indeed, its decorators seem to have had no control over colors or trimmings. The more color, the more gilt, the more carving, the richer the result. There was a sense of suffocation and dust in those old Pullman cars. Young people of today have happily never known the combination of plush curtains and soot from open windows. There were elaborate patterns on everything, even on the parts of berths that were turned toward the wall. The windows were draped with curtains, edged with fringe, and tied back with tassels.

Bok, with his usual joy in combat, started a campaign against the ugliness and dirt. The Pullman Company ignored him. They thought their cars the epitome of beauty and luxury. Furthermore, the Pullman Company had more business than it knew what to do with. Passengers had to wait their turn for accommodations. Why should they spend a lot of money for a silly notion in a ladies' magazine? But the railroads, who didn't own the Pullman cars supported Bok.

Soon, Pullman conductors reported that the passengers were join-
ing the chorus of criticism. The Pullman Company was annoyed.
Then Bok engaged two well known architects, had them draw up
suggested changes in the design of the Pullman cars and passed
their ideas on to the railroad companies. The tide turned suddenly
when the Chicago, Burlington and Quincy Railroad burst out with
a new dining car. According to Bok, it was an "artistically treated
Flemish-oak-paneled car with longitudinal beams and cross beams,
giving the impression of a ceiling-beamed room. There were quiet
tones of deep yellow and no carving. The whole tone of the car
was that of the rich color of the sunflower." Slowly the germ-laden
plush and velvet disappeared, giving way to leather hangings,
"beautiful and simple and easy to keep clean." They were still
ugly, however.

Bok won this fight, but he lost the next one. He says that it was
"only a step from the Pullman car to the landscape outside." He
therefore set out to get rid of billboards, a truly giant battle. How
unsuccessful he was, anyone with eyes can see today. But he
fought hard, and in doing so, gave an enormous boost to the power
of women. Without quite realizing it, he taught them how to organize that power, so that today we women are able to get our
ungloved hands into everything.

Bok had piles of photographs made of the screaming advertising
horrors and published them in the *Ladies' Home Journal*. He got
the women's clubs and other civic outfits busy, and began to talk
about legal control of the use of billboards. He offered prizes for
sets of photos in pairs, one showing a fence, a barn or a field with
billboard and the other, the same spot without a billboard, with
the affidavit of the owner, stating there had been a billboard and
that he had removed it. Of course advertisers threatened the *Ladies'
Home Journal*, but no account was actually withdrawn from the
magazine.

It all really got nowhere or little-where. Bok did get rid of a huge billboard at Niagara Falls and "the largest sign in the world," which was about to be placed on the rim of the Grand Canyon. Some state legislators even talked about regulations, which would not prohibit billboards, but keep them in reasonable bounds. It really was a fine try of Bok's, and though it failed, it led him on to a bigger fight.

As he traveled about the country on the billboard campaign, he came across many of the sore spots, sore to the eye, and because of dirt and poor sanitation, to health. He began a bold series in the *Journal* called "Dirty Cities." He chose Lynn, Massachusetts, as his first example. Lynn rose in fury, screamed that the attack was in bad taste. But local pride took over and Lynn did some house-cleaning.

Trenton, New Jersey, came next and Wilkes-Barre, Pennsylvania, was the third. In both, there was first anger, then some clean-up. Memphis followed, but in Memphis there were no outbursts of anger, and the general feeling was that Bok had done the city a service.

And so it went. The return in publicity for the magazine was tremendous. But in the long run, it was just a rinsing of the dirt, not a scouring. It couldn't be more, because nothing fundamental about the cities was brought out. It couldn't be, because Bok himself hadn't a notion of the reason for the dirt in the cities. No deep-seated cure was effected. For instance in Lynn, Massachusetts, nothing was said about the long lines of dark and ugly cotton mills.

Most of the clean-up work was done by the women and their organizations. It was a profound lesson in power. Bok understood women well, and he fed their vanity and pride. I don't mean that women had never done any public do-gooding before. Even as far back as 1828, Sarah Hale had organized efforts to help sailors' wives. But Bok did the thing on a large scale. None of the move-ments he started were basic, but they showed women what they could do; how they could put their manicured fingers into the pie and help him pull out a fine publicity plum, and maybe do a little good, too.

The gentle style with an undertone of iron command which was characteristic of Sarah Josepha Hale was brought to ripe fruition by Bok. Words were soft, they were not often used clearly or sharply, they should be "smooth, round and slippery." The edges should be rubbed off, so that, if a reader loved the sound of words like peace, goodness, etc., she would not be offended by too close an examination of the author's commands and real objectives.

Margaret Sangster, who wrote for the *Ladies' Home Journal* for many years, and later, for many other years, for the *Woman's Home Companion,* was a star performer in producing this style. She said in the *Ladies' Home Journal* in 1892:

Lady was made to be the title of such women as she, dignified, courteous, with manners that may well be called finished, so they are touched with a gentle ceremony, so they are free from haste, and rounded out with leisure. *Woman* is a term for business and service, for everyday use and wont. *Lady* may be defined as "Woman in a high state of civilization . . ." my beautiful, great lady, in her lustreless gown of rich black silk, with yellow ruffles at her wrists, and her antique brooch at her throat.

Don't make any mistake, Mrs. Sangster was no softie, however this may sound. And as we have seen and shall see even more later on, Bok was a tough fighter, though he never used a hard nut of a word. He was able to announce in 1891, two years after he took over, that the *Ladies' Home Journal* had the largest circulation of any magazine in the world. The subscription price was still one dollar a year, single copies ten cents. But there were many reduced price offers, such as the magazine combined with a book. One such offer was a pathetic effort on Bok's part to educate and improve the reading taste of his public. He offered *Paradise Lost,* Dickens, Scott and Macaulay. Alas, his public said no, preferring *East Lynne.*

Advertising rates would make the modern advertiser sigh: three dollars an agate line in preferred positions. It was general usage then to run ads disguised as reading matter, which no reputable magazine would do today. The price for this was five dollars a line. (The price of a page today is roughly, in the *Ladies' Home Journal,* black and white, $22,650; a four-color page, $30,000.)

Bok used his magazine to preach, to exhort, to order, to improve taste, to clean up the slums. But he never forgot that all this was just jam and peanut butter. The bread for which women paid their dollar a year was the solid information they could use . . . the household, the cooking, the fashions. And for these, especially the household and cooking, Bok employed the best people he could. There were three household editors, Miss Maria Parloa, Mrs. Janet McKenzie and Mrs. S. T. Rorer. They were all famous cooks, and shrewd, capable housekeepers.

Their information was good and they had a clear field. The mountains of recipes which have bombarded us these last years, had not appeared. Little information had been published on how to make housekeeping easier and cheaper and better, and the housekeeper needed help, needed advice. In one issue in 1896 there was a weekly program suggesting how housework should be arranged. This was for Monday:

Rise at five A.M. and wash one or two boilers of clothes. Prepare and serve breakfast. [Not just orange juice and coffee, you can be sure.] After breakfast, clean table, put away food, put dishes to soak, air chambers and bedding. Finish washing. Wash dishes and clean kitchen. Prepare midday meal. Bathe; put on a loose wrapper and rest for an hour or two. After resting, take the clothes from the line and fold. Prepare supper. Retire early.

Reading the above program, it is easy to understand one woman who told Bok, "I believe the happiest hour of a woman's life is her last."

However, the household woman got a break in the number and the cheapness of "hired girls." Bok gave a lot of space to the subject. In September, 1892, alone, there were five pieces, entitled:

> "Between Mistress and Maid"
> "The Evolution of the Hired Girl"
> "Who Are Our Best Servants?"
> "Untruthfulness of Servants"
> "Recommendations of Servants"

Under the "Evolution of the Hired Girl," Harriet Prescott Spofford wrote:

Fifty years ago, where slavery did not obtain, we relied for our domestic service on the children of the old freed slaves, on the needy among our country people, and complaints about servants were unheard. The women of the house, whatever their wealth, aided largely in the conduct of affairs, and the young girls of small means, or no means at all, graduated from the kitchen into marriage.

When immigration from Ireland began, life was still so simple that no one recognized the enormous changes which that was to bring. The housekeepers could now procure a pair of hands for the drudgery at FIFTY CENTS A WEEK. [All capitals here are used as in the original, an indication of the gushy style.] When the drudge became better accomplished, she received seventy-five cents a week and sometimes a dollar. Until some time after 1850, a dollar and a half a week was considered handsome wages. On this capital, these servants imported a whole generation of Irish boys and girls. Supply created the demand: for many individuals who had always done their own work had found someone else to do it.

Meanwhile our own young people, released from the kitchens, went one step higher in entering factories and shops. The daughters of the house, too, set free from domestic duties, had the time for books and music and general cultivation, and a wave of culture swept over the land in the wake of these Irish girls that leaves us owing them an unpayable debt.

It does not need that the culture should be of the deepest or highest; such as it is, it is an advance in the direction of the deepest and highest, and in large measure it is a consequence of the leisure that the Irish immigration has made for us.

With the Civil War wages of servants rose with the prices of all commodities, so that the AVERAGE COOK COMMANDS FIVE DOLLARS A WEEK, and of a superior sort, yet far below rank of a CHEF, receives EIGHT. Indeed when we recount what our homes would be like without her labors, so far from quarrelling with the price paid, we feel like giving them an increase; and when we picture the scene of desolation a kitchen presents to a girl who descends to light the fire on cold mornings, we feel that the utmost consideration we can give her is not enough.

Harriet Spofford, however, was speaking for a more limited portion of the American public than she realized. It is true that a family of six could live with sunshine and space and good food, but no luxuries, on fifteen dollars a week. But such a family couldn't afford to pay even fifty cents a week for a maid. Americans never enjoyed the services of servants and domestics in the degree to which Europeans were already accustomed. Even in the middle-class families that could afford servants, they usually could not until after a number of years of marriage, so that the wife had to be educated on how to choose and how to treat a servant.

Mrs. Lyman Abbott, under the title, "Who are Our Best Servants?," gave the following advice:

The sturdy German girl for much drudgery.

Where hours are irregular, and where the housemother needs sympathy . . . the warm-hearted Irish.

For loyalty and conscientious attention to duty . . . the Scotch cannot be surpassed.

I find it much better to take my servants into a sort of partnership . . . letting them know when circumstances call for extra work. We must not forget that (whatever the nationality of our domestics) we are all one family and one in our Father.

There were plenty of girls to be had for housework; there was little else they could get to do. Factory jobs paid about two dollars and fifty cents a week in New York City; and there were some, but very few, salesgirls in the stores. In the more important departments men stood behind the counters. But new jobs for women were coming along over the horizon, and Bok knew it. He still regarded women highly, not as statuettes, but as human beings . . . thinking, working beings. He was ahead of his time in his attitude toward women, although we can hardly expect him to be of our time. For instance, in 1891 the *Journal* said that women could support themselves on less money than men but that didn't mean that their work was worth less. And that because she "was regarded with appreciation" by men didn't mean that she should receive less pay. Very forward-looking for 1891. But he'd rather they didn't work "in business."

The atmosphere of commercial life has never been conducive to the best interests of women engaged in it. The number of women in business who lose their gentleness and womanliness is far greater than those who retain what, after all, are woman's best and chief qualities. To be in an office where there are only men has never yet done a single girl any good; and it has done harm to thousands . . . I know whereof I speak, and I deal not in generalities.

The *Journal* suggested as possible jobs the stage, dressmaking, art, medicine, teaching, typesetting, telegraphy, stenography, but with a special emphasis on nursing.

In 1892 came a whisper of something that didn't really come along fully until 1910. Virginia Frazee wrote:

Among occupations offered to women, nine out of ten are overcrowded or not at all suited to the women of literary bent. But to the suggestion: "Become a writer of advertisement," the bread-seeker is apt to reply: "Why I never thought of that."

Of course not; very few women have thought of it and that is why it is a good thing to think of it now. This is a comparatively new occupation offering great inducements, especially to the woman of literary aspirations.

One woman writes three advertisements a week, each of one hundred lines—one for shoes, one for jewelry, one for dry goods. Each pays her fifteen dollars—making her weekly earnings forty-five dollars.

Another woman writes catchy jingles—rhymes on various lines of business—$1500 or $2,000 considered good pay for the first year or two.

Why does not the woman artist try making illustrations for dry goods literature? This is a profession brimful of possibilities for the woman who is capable of doing it.

All this appeared under a banner heading, reading: "In Literary Circles." That was sixty-eight years ago, and colleges are still pouring out boys and girls who think advertising is one facet of literature.

A writer named Ruth Ashmore dropped some pretty harsh "hints" for money-making (*Ladies' Home Journal*—1891):

I am not a believer in girls going out in the world to work unless it is absolutely necessary. But when it is, then I want them to do it in the right way: I want them to think that every particle of work they do, is done not only for their own sakes, not only for their employers—it must be right and honest in the sight of God. As Ruskin said: "Queens you should always be. Queens to your lovers, to your husbands, to your sons; queens of a higher mystery to the world beyond."

And Miss Ashmore winds up with some familiar-sounding words about the girls who, five minutes before the hour, get ready to leave the office:

The woman who announces she must work or starve, and yet is not willing to be at her desk at eight o'clock in the morning, deserves to starve.

Bok's campaign to make women aware of themselves did not stop with investigation of the household and the job possibilities; he began to look into the premises on which American marriages were founded. The opinions and propaganda of the *Ladies' Home Journal* were naturally not of one piece. Some of the contributors were harsher and more outspoken than Bok. Not everyone knew how to manipulate the velvet glove as well as he did. For example, take Ella Wheeler Wilcox, in October, 1891, under the heading "Social Slave Markets:"

I have heard and read so much during the past four years on the subject of our social slave markets, that I have set myself the task of looking into the matter. By the slave market I mean the marriage system of society in the home.

Though put more toughly than Bok would have said it, this was really part of his efforts to "set women free," a policy that lurked behind everything in the magazine.

However, the conception seems slightly confused when we read this by the Rev. Charles H. Parkhurst, a very unclean-minded-do-gooder. It comes in 1896 under the heading of "Marrying for Money:"

A poor young man, marrying a poor young girl, with only the prospect that their life will become more and more complicated as time goes on, is a fool. I have had affectionate couples wait upon me to be married and then ask me to trust them for the wedding fee. I think that we who are clergymen should refuse to marry applicants who cannot show to our satisfaction that there is no likelihood that either they or their poor offspring will ever come upon the town.

Then he goes on to caution his readers against marrying for money. Slightly muddled, but apparently if you had his fee, you were on the right road.

There is a good deal about manners, naturally, but we can hardly afford to condescend to them. Etiquette continued to be a sure-fire best seller. In an 1892 issue, the *Ladies' Home Journal Treasury* finds this: "It is very crude to eat on the streets." Nothing about chewing gum or smoking by ladies on the street. Or carrying bundles. It was assumed in that day of much menial service that no lady ever carried a bundle on the street. However, there was a limit to the menial service, an area in which the personal touch was still needed, as in these quotes from early issues:

> She always washed her dress herself, as her mother had before her.

> I never allow a servant to touch my fine china.

> This card table (at which Washington sat) is never polished by a housemaid. I rub it myself or my daughter does it for me.

The etiquette of calling cards was especially rigid, "The turned down corner signifying a personal visit is obsolete." However, "When men send out invitations . . . an entertainment at his studio, on board his yacht or elsewhere, the ladies who have accepted his hospitality send his cards shortly afterward by messenger, bearing a few words of appreciative thanks."

By 1908, however, etiquette had begun to contain a new kind of information, highly indicative of the change that Bok was bringing about in the lives of women. From the *Ladies' Home Journal* of November, 1908:

> What Forty Business Girls Have Found Out.

> I begin my Christmas letters in October, which gives me ample time to make each letter interesting.

A small square of oilcloth under the office chair saves my skirt from dirt and wear.

An office girl should not stick her hair full of lead pencils.

On sloppy days I line the backs of my shoes with newspaper where my wet skirt strikes them.

The best office apron is black sateen.

By 1908, when this article was written, women were commonplace in smaller jobs, though it was still impossible for a woman to get a copy-writing job in an advertising agency. One of the first was Helen Lansdowne, later Mrs. Stanley Resor, who got her job in 1910. I think I was the second, in 1912.

Simultaneously, as women moved out into the world, came the first indications of concern. "Freedom for women is fine, but Are Our Girls Too Independent?" asked Mrs. Frank Leslie, an independent and successful business woman. She said in March, 1892:

Girls of today no more need a chaperone than their grandmothers did, but as in foreign society no girl must be seen unchaperoned, and Mrs. Grundy says: "My girls are just as valuable as anybody else's girls, and if the others have chaperones, so shall mine."

But the problem was becoming evident. A piece on "Promiscuous Bathing" by Felicia Holt, described with horror a daring innovation on the beaches:

Not content with the snugly fitting white serge skirt and blouse, revealing every curve, milady must now wear stockings that expose the toes!

One thing that was worrying the guardians of purity was the growing craze for the bicycle and the fashion for ankle-length skirts that came with it. *Holiday* for July, 1948, said that between

1890 and 1896, Americans spent $100,000,000 for bicycles. As a result:

In 1896 the watch and jewelry business was all but defunct; piano business was off fifty per cent; furniture men were pleading with young ladies to stop buying bicycles with their parlor-set savings, and saloon-keepers were growling that the bicycle was taking bread out of their mouths.

Saddle horse and carriage firms were closing up. A prominent hat manufacturer in desperation, demanded that Congress pass a law requiring every cyclist to buy two felt hats a year, whether he wore them or not. Cigar sales were off a million a day, and shoe-makers, according to that report, sat idle, "since" they said, "hardly anyone walks any longer."

One unnamed book-and-periodical dealer in New York City was quoted as saying his business was off a million dollars a year. Most pathetic of all were the barbers; after a day's work, they complained, their customers went out cycling, instead of getting a shave and dressing up, adding, "When a man skips a shave today, we can't sell him two shaves tomorrow . . . that shave is gone forever."

The impact of the bicycle on women's fashions was equally impressive. Before bicycles came along, women's skirts were like huge brooms, sweeping the streets. By 1897, the fashion for ankle-length skirts had reached the high schools for everyday use. Girls no longer had to carry a heavy load of books in one arm and hold up their skirts with the other hand. Those first bicycle skirts were made of a thick material with eight or nine rows of stitching around the bottom. They were a great relief and the elegant high-school girl now had merely to work on her stiff pompadour, worn over a "rat," her many petticoats, her gloves and her veil.

Other fashions had the same over-decoration as those described in the *Delineator* in the eighties. But something was added: the bustle. The bustle was as bold a sexual symbol as the skin tight shorts of today. And talking about sex, there was an odd fashion

Sara Josepha Hale, the first lady persuader

He published the "Lady's Book"—Louis Antoine Godey

An early attempt at emancipation—bicycling pantaloons for young ladies!

POPPING THE QUESTION
(A woman's right)

The words in the balloon read: "My dear Theophilis! Can you reject a heart which will ever throb with the fondest affection for you? a hand which will ever be raised to protect your spotless innocence?"

"Well, I'll ask Ma."

In 1960 writer Jessica Mitford gives us a modern proposal in her autobiography:

"Esmond, are you planning to go back to Spain?" I asked.

"Yes, I think I'll be leaving again in a week or so."

No point beating about the bush—it was now or never . . .

"Well—I was wondering if you could possibly take me with you."

"Yes, I could, but don't let's talk about it now," he answered, glancing round to see if anyone was listening.

The road sign in this picture captioned "Sweet Liberty" reads "To The Great City." One must give these tempters credit; they did little to try to fool the girls.

Office scene, end of the 19th Century; or, in the mind of the beholder, "a seduction scene."

This little thing played a huge part in freeing women from a lot of snobbish nonsense, at least as far as dress was concerned.

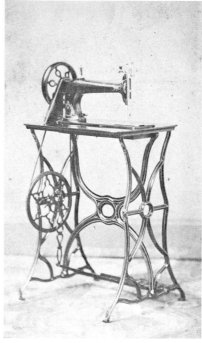

Yours for Health
Lydia E. Pinkham

Lydia E. Pinkham, whose vegetable compound was a boon to womanhood.

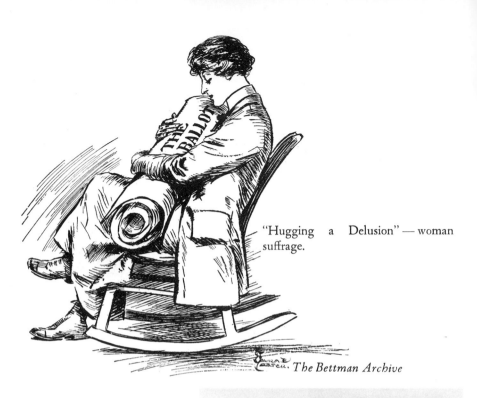

"Hugging a Delusion" — woman suffrage.

For generations Fannie Merritt Farmer showed women how to make food taste good. Her recipes are good to this day, though others may be more photogenic.

PICTORIAL REVIEW

MARCH 1926

FIFTEEN CENTS

Culver Service

Edward W. Bok, editor of The *Ladies Home Journal*. He laid new roads which other women's magazines followed for years and more or less still follow. He began with high ideals about women; he saw his mother and grandmother in them all. But when he retired after thirty years, he refused to say what he thought of them.

What is taste? And what is beauty? In the eyes of Bok this house was a dream of loveliness. It belonged to Louis Tiffany, one of the owners of the jewelry firm. It was actually a grim, heavy affair. Children were afraid to pass it on their way across 72nd Street to New York's Central Park.

Even in babies and children, fashions change. In 1910 young mothers swore by Dr. Emmett Holt. Today they have the good sense to swear by Dr. Benjamin Spock.

Dr. Harvey Wiley. *Good Housekeeping* owes the reputation of its Good Housekeeping Institute to him. But it would be interesting to hear his forthright comments if he could see it now.

Gertrude Lane, for over thirty years editor of *The Woman's Home Companion*. She looked rather mousey. Her manner was gentle, her voice soft. And she tried never to say a flat *yes* or *no*. In short, she was a lady. But under that exterior she was a strong, tough woman who didn't much like men.

The elegant Edna Woolman Chase, for many years Editor-in-Chief of *Vogue*. She had charm, intelligence and a sense of fashion. She was two different people. In her job she played "a great lady," driving up to her office in her car, followed to the elevator by her chauffeur, carrying some silly little package. But in private life she was often simple, charming, and devoid of any chi-chi.

Finchley

Unique Among America's Finest Shops

TOGETHERNESS

"His" & "Her" Companion Hats

A SMART, COLOURFUL DELIGHTFUL IDEA TO EXCITE CONVERSATION AT PARTIES, AT THE CLUB, POOL OR JUST DASHING ABOUT TOWN IN YOUR CONVERTIBLE.

Fine White Thomas Cotton accented with multi-coloured roman stripings

Men's	*Ladies'*
Sizes, 6⅞ to 7½	*Sizes S. M. L.*
$5	**$4**

FREE STORAGE
Any make of felt hat left for complete renovation stored free of charge until Fall. Old hats made to look like new by expert hatters. **$7.50**

Order by Mail or Telephone, JU 2-3230

Open Thursday Evenings until 8:30 P.M.

564 Fifth Ave. at 46th St., N. Y. (36) :: 19 E. Jackson Blvd., Chicago (4)

Culver Service

McCall's pushed the idea of "Togetherness," and pushed and pushed until it reached such absurdities as this ad for the usually dignified firm of Finchley.

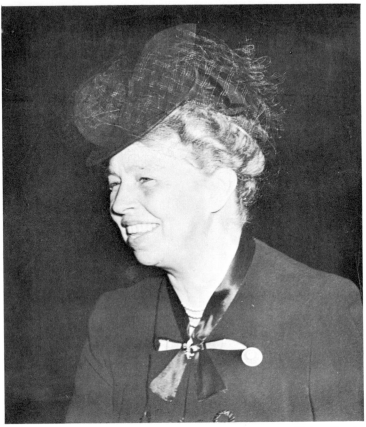

Culver Service

She persuades the Lady Persuaders

mentioned in the *Ladies' Home Journal* of 1891: The masher's coat
. . . fitted overvest effect.

Old people had a real place then, and Margaret Sangster wrote
a series of sensible articles about them in the matter of keeping
young. Elderly women, she said, should dress daintily, and old
people resent too much care. This was kindly and sensible but the
slop-over into mush could apparently not be avoided, as in expressions like "keeping the child heart."

On the subject of food, those old *Ladies' Home Journals* were
superb. The field was fresh and there was plenty of material to
choose from. The women who wrote on food were good. Mrs.
Rorer had a famous restaurant in Philadelphia and another on
Broad Street in New York, where the trimmings were plain: just
fine linens, lots of room betweeen the tables, and perfect food.

In the pages of the *Ladies' Home Journal,* these women wrote
about *food,* not only about something to serve. Of course they
didn't know some things we know; and they made boners, like
this:

Fruits should be used sparingly for children under three, especially
bananas. After a year old, if your baby is in perfect health, he may have
a teaspoonful of orange juice occasionally.

I lectured once at a university with an elaborate domestic science
school. I was guided through the kitchens. Never in my life have
I seen such beautiful, modern and efficient equipment. After that,
the President and the Dean, several of the teachers, four prize
cooking students and I sat down to lunch. Nice looking table.
Correct and even elegant setting. Then the meal: canned fruit
cocktail, two large greasy veal chops; the salad was sweet with a
thick bottled mayonnaise and the dessert was ice cream with
crackers out of a box. There was just one good item . . . the
ice cream which was made in the kitchen. Canned fruit and

crackers out of a box are all right in their place, but this was a demonstration of the cooking skills of the pupils and of the efficiency of the equipment. It showed only the skill of a can-opener and a frying pan. The meal had been prepared by young women who were going out into the world to plan food for schools, hospitals and hotels, and who, worse luck, were going to teach other girls how to cook.

And all this is not because we don't know enough about food, but too much of the wrong things. In the nineties they didn't know enough or have enough machines to get up a meal like that. Another thing they didn't have then was perfect color photography for food. That didn't come through until the 1920's. Photogenic food isn't always good to eat. Vitamins and calories are important, goodness knows, but alas, they have become more important than the taste and quality of what we eat. Science has fought with the cook at the old kitchen stove. Science has won. It has won so completely that much of our American cooking now comes out of an antiseptic laboratory instead of a warm, human kitchen.

Bok's efforts to educate the American public continued. He next tried to keep people from being victimized by false advertising claims. It was a lush time for the patent medicine cure-alls. Even the most respectable publications pushed such nostrums in their advertising pages. The only periodicals left out of the bonanza were those whose readers knew too much.

One of the most virulent cure-alls was Lydia Pinkham's Pink Pills for Pale People. I'd like to quote something I wrote for *The American Mercury* some years ago:

> The woman of her day was almost vulgarly modest. She would rather die than go to a male doctor with her various "female" troubles. The idea of being examined thoroughly by a gynecologist would have filled her with horror. Even having a baby delivered by a man seemed a disgusting

invasion of privacy. It seemed even worse to the husbands of the time. Hence the wide employment of the midwife.

Mrs. Pinkham diagnosed hardening of the kidneys, ulcers of the right ovary, weakened ligaments of the left side of the womb—all without even seeing the patients.

Lydia was not really a fraud. She was simply able to live cozily with two completely contradictory ideas: that alcohol was evil, and that women must be saved by her Pink Pills, which were themselves loaded with alcohol.

The Pink Pills were so widely used that they were grist for the wits of the time. One song went:

> Mrs. Simpson had no breastworks,
> She could hardly wear a blouse
> Till she took some Lydia Pinkham's—
> Now they milk her with the cows!

To Bok, none of this was funny, and he fought Lydia with all he had. But it had as much effect as a powder puff hitting a goose-feather pillow. For instance, he quoted one of her ads:

Mrs. Pinkham in her laboratory at Lynn, Massachusetts, is able to do more for the ailing women of America than the family physician. Any woman, therefore, is responsible for her own suffering who will not take the trouble to write to Mrs. Pinkham for advice.

Next to the reproduction of this advertisement, Bok simply placed a photograph of Mrs. Pinkham's tombstone in Pine Grove Cemetery at Lynn, showing that she had died twenty years before. While she was supposed to be diagnosing the poor, sick, and foolish, she had been lying "moldering in the grave."

But Mrs. Pinkham was backed by a powerful moneyed group

ready to fight with weapons as dirty as their medicines. Their business ran into the hundreds of millions of dollars, and they had no intention of allowing the editor of a magazine to endanger that business. They showered Congress with propaganda and tried to reach key congressional leaders with bribery; also state legislators and physicians' organizations, to whom they paid big sums for endorsements for their patent medicines. It was this same moneyed group which, later, so bitterly opposed Dr. Harvey Wiley. (The patent medicine chicanery still goes on, but under different guises, some entirely respectable).

But even as Bok was losing his battle against Lydia Pinkham, he extended his attacks against all patent medicines which seemed to him either dangerous or useless. "Soothing syrup given to a teething baby contains morphine," charged Bok. He quoted a physician who testified that he had known at least six children directly killed by their parents with soothing syrup.

"A certain cod liver oil essence for children made them incurable alcoholics," warned Bok.

"A headache cure for women contains a dangerous amount of chloroform."

"Vegetable Extract contains 41-6/10 per cent alcohol."

Burning with anger, Bok started the greatest crusade of his career. He announced that after 1892, the *Ladies' Home Journal* would take no more patent medicine advertising. This was a tremendous risk, since in one issue alone, January, 1891, there had been ads of the following: Dr. Sage's Catarrh Remedy, Dr. Steel's Tooth Preservative, Paralysis Cured—and many more.

Bok's blast bewildered many simple-minded readers who had an almost religious faith in their bottles of cure. Many a dedicated teetotaler had been getting a pleasant lift from her innocent bottle of alcohol, especially with all its fine testimonials from important people. Bok exposed false testimonials for patent medicine from

Senators and Congressmen. He showed up a Washington journalist who charged seventy-five dollars for a Senator's endorsement and forty dollars for a Congressman's. But Bok could not halt the march of the Frankenstein monster, advertising, which he had helped to create. Testimonials continued, increased in number, and they were no more (and probably little less) truthful than those given today. Henry Ward Beecher gave one to the Erie Railroad and Sir Erasmus Wilson, the first and only president of the Royal College of Surgeons who ever gave a public testimonial, said: Soap is to the skin what wine is to the stomach.

Bok soon found that his crusade against patent medicines was failing. He himself was being attacked. Other magazines, newspapers, and even clergymen went after him heartily. Advertisers thinking "who next?" canceled ads.

The *Ladies' Home Journal* lost more than its patent medicine ads, as the pressure mounted from all sides. But back of Bok's brashness was an iron will. He engaged Mark Sullivan, a young lawyer, persuaded him to give up his practice and put his full time into the war on the nostrums. Mark Sullivan did such a brilliant job for Bok, and later for *Collier's Weekly,* that he became known as one of the leading journalists of America.

One of the meanest scandals that Sullivan exposed was this: Thousands of women wrote to the nostrum people about their complaints as though they were consulting doctors. Then, the patent medicine scum in turn sold the letters to anyone who would buy them. Some of the material that Sullivan dug up was too strong for Bok's still lady-like magazine, and Sullivan went on with the campaign in *Collier's Weekly.* From that time on, however, Sullivan, Samuel Hopkins Adams, *Collier's* and the *Ladies' Home Journal* all joined in the campaign to stop the patent medicine racket. Other periodicals came along, until finally the public woke up and Congress passed the Pure Food and Drug Act. Now, interstate advertising is carefully watched. False advertising has not been entirely eliminated, but has been driven to disguise itself with ambiguity.

In 1906, Lyman Abbott, a famous clergyman, suggested to Bok that he carry out a similar campaign against venereal diseases. At first, Bok thought this had nothing to do with the home or the family, but a little investigation woke him up. He talked it over with his friends, who all said, "Don't!" Cyrus Curtis alone stood by him. They both realized that they might lose circulation because of such articles, probably as many as 100,000 readers. Bok, however, decided to go further than merely to make his readers aware of the dangers of venereal diseases; he wanted to rid the American people of their hush-hush attitude toward childbirth.

Bok's theory was that parents must tell children the truth about "the mystery of life." Of course he wrapped it up in the usual jelly-like language of the day. But that he did it at all at that time took immense courage. He explained that he would not "tell the actual story of the beginning of life" in the magazine. He put that responsibility up to the parents. He warned them that the articles would keep on, and that there would be many of them, and that if a reader didn't approve, she had better stop the magazine at once.

Bok said later that "he had the grim experience of seeing his magazine, hitherto proclaimed all over the land as a model advocate of the virtues, refused admittance into thousands of homes. He saw his own friends tear the offending pages out of the periodical before it was allowed to find a place on their home tables."

Bok got some highly respectable writers to contribute articles to his campaign, hoping in that way to win approval. But after about a year and a half he had to give it up. It was getting nowhere and it cost the *Ladies' Home Journal* plenty.

Another campaign in which he had limited success was his effort to put the bathroom inside the house. We find it difficult today to understand the resistance which he met. Though Bok did his best to explain both the functions and the value of having the bathroom inside the house, many of his readers remained puzzled about how and how much they should be used. Rural people in particular could see no convenience in having the bathroom inside. Bok had to resort to all kinds of persuasion, to take his campaign to a moral level, using the "cleanliness next to godliness" approach.

In 1896 there was an editorial headed: "The Morals of the Bathroom," in which Bok tried to point out a direct connection between cleanliness of people and their moral standards.

The Dutch are the cleanest people in the world. Holland is also the most moral nation, according to statistics. The average American man is a busy creature—he is apt to be neglectful of smaller things—generally takes the form of neglect of personal habits.

And then a statement which will astonish the elegencia of today. "The better the appearance of our men the higher will be the standard of morality."

But Cyrus Edson, M.D., ex-President of the New York Board of Health, has more precise guidance; he was worried about open pores. "A child (aged one to ten years) should be bathed in a tub once a week. Between ten and fifteen, children should not bathe more than twice a week (though of course a sponge bath should be taken every day). Once a week is sufficient for cleanliness, less than that is not."

The opinions and propaganda of the *Journal* were naturally not of one piece. It can be seen that Bok, as well as some of the other contributors to his magazine gave such curious advice as:

"I certainly wouldn't want to recommend to you any of Tolstoy's books. Nobody ever gained by looking on the dark side of everything."

Or this fashion note: "Large leghorn hats are not suited, save on very small people, for church." (That calls up a very odd picture indeed. We see a procession of mushrooms on short stems, filing into the pews.)

Needless to say the attitude towards morals was grave, not to say severe. But certain aspects, like the attitude to the drinking of wine, are somewhat confusing to the modern, who doesn't think much about polite drinking of wine, but of "winos" and alcoholism.

In 1892 there was a discussion in the *Journal* on the question of whether the use (sic) of wine at social functions was decreasing. Opinions varied. John Wanamaker, whose weakness lay in other directions than alcohol, believed that there was an advance toward moderation in wine drinking. He wrote:

From personal experience, unable to give any information, but I am told that the use of wines and liquors for social purposes is not in proportion to the increase in population at large dinner parties. Many guests do not use liquors, while at receptions lemonade has replaced punch in many households. I am led to believe that much of this moderation is due to temperance agitation and to the abundance and increased use of mineral waters.

President Rutherford B. Hayes, whose wife refused to serve any alcoholic liquor in the White House, said that he was not confident there was a decline. Mrs. Edna Payne Whitney, wife of the ex-Secretary of State, talked of "fashion of temperance" and "hygienic tendencies" and thought that mothers need not worry about that temptation for their sons.

Another contributor paints a gruesome picture. Or maybe you'd call it an elegant picture:

Without undertaking to handle the moral aspect . . . look, for example, at the large parties, which, at half after one in the afternoon, are convened, ladies in visiting costume, bonneted and veiled, to be shut in a darkened dining room, where gas and candles supplant the wholesome light of day. There during two mortal hours . . . cucumbers, caviar, truffles, pâté de fois gras, almonds, mayonnaise . . . just a portion to the addenda of the feast. To relieve the thirst thus engendered, the banqueteer has recourse to what? Besides her plate stands the same array of glasses—of English cut—of Venice or gilded Carlsbad ware, lending glitter or color to the board—glasses for sherry, Rhine wine, for claret, for champagne, all that would be demanded for the most formal dinner.

One of Edward Bok's campaigns was against Paris fashions. He had clothes designed in this country and showed them in his magazine. Bok thought American women ought to wear American fashions. He demanded that the "American woman come out from under the yoke of the French couturiers to show her patriotism." It turned out that the American woman would cheerfully sacrifice her patriotism. She would even justify a possible disregard of the decencies. All for a "Paris model." So in this effort too Bok was defeated.

Among his targets were falsely labeled French models, but he says, "Within a year after the *Journal* stopped the campaign, baffled and beaten, the trade in French labels was greater than ever. Hundreds of French models that had never crossed the ocean were sold, the American woman was being hoodwinked on every hand, and the reign of the French couturier was once more supreme."

Bok was due for an even bigger disappointment. He tried to stop the use of the aigrette, the beautiful feather of the egret, as a trimming for hats. He showed, by photograph and text, how in order to get an aigrette, it was necessary to let the mother bird die slowly, leaving a nest of baby birds to starve. This was the only time she produced such a feather. Bok not only failed in this campaign against aigrettes, but was astounded to find that the demand for the feather had more than quadrupled. He says in his *Autobiography* that he had dwelt on the aigrette as a mark of wealth and fashion and on how expensive it was. As a consequence women regarded it as the top in adornment. Thousands of women who had never before known these things made up their minds to own an aigrette at any price.

He could not believe what he heard. He talked to milliners, to buyers, and then to his own women friends, and he quotes what one of them told him: "Take my own case. You will doubtless be shocked when I tell you that I was perfectly aware of the conditions under which the aigrette is obtained before you began your exposure of the method. But did it prevent my purchase of one? Not at all. Why? Because I am a woman. I realize that no head ornament will set off my hair as well as an aigrette. Say I am cruel if you like. I wish the heron-mother didn't have to be killed and the babies starve, but, Mr. Bok, I must have my beautiful aigrette!"

Bok refused to give up. He engaged lawyers, he had bills drawn up, and he traveled to talk personally to legislators. He tried to have the bills passed quietly, but word of his efforts got about. Women, afraid that they might never have another chance to buy an aigrette, for a time increased the demand. But this time Bok won, because the United States Congress, made up of men, passed a Federal Law at the urging of the Audubon Society.

But Bok says, talking of himself as usual in the third person, "his ideal of womanhood has received a severe jolt. He was conscious that something had toppled off its pedestal which never could be replaced."

When he became editor of the *Journal,* his mother had said: "I am sorry you are going to take this position. It will cost you the high ideal you have always held of your mother's sex. But a nature, as is the feminine nature, wholly swayed inwardly by emotion and outwardly influenced by an insatiate love for personal adornment, will never stand the analysis you will give it."

And that no doubt was why Bok, after his retirement, refused to tell newspapermen what he thought about women.

But Bok had trained women to a realization of their power. He had, by using the feather-dusting style of writing, put across some powerful ideas. He had flattered his readers, he had scolded them, he had endlessly advised and commanded them. He had taught them to use their power in an organized fashion.

The editorial patterns he set are still being used today. There have been minor departures, like the methods of *Good Housekeeping*. There have been specializations, as magazines for the young, one for parents, some for brides, for businesswomen, for working women, for this and that, and there's a new line about sex. But the tone and the methods are still those begun by Sarah Hale and perfected by Bok. How they are struggling in that boa constrictor of traditions is part of their later story.

In the years from 1919 to 1935, after Bok retired, the *Journal* tried to follow his editorial pattern. But what came through was weak and uncertain. Searching for another Bok, the *Journal* used a stream of editors. Bok had published what he himself liked and that happened to be what millions of women also liked. Those who followed him as editors were working on guess and speculation. They tried to guess what Bok might have done, or else speculate on what the public might like.

By 1935, during the depression years, the editors were quite lost. Like all other women's magazines the *Journal* insisted on turning a rosy face on the economy and as a consequence treated the depression pretty casually. Just here and there one found a suggestion for economical living, as in the following nonsense

about a design for a small house "with a studio living room"—
this at a time when people could barely pay for any living space,
much less for a studio living room.

Right along the *Journal* had been selling patterns for houses at
one dollar each. These designs contained complete architect's plans,
a quantity survey of materials, architect's specifications for materials
and workmanship. It also included a cardboard cut-out of a model
house.

Absent from all this was a most important item, the matter
of getting mortgages on houses in the suburbs and especially in
the country. In this the *Journal* was like all the other women's
magazines. All of them then, before, and since have been prolific
in ideas about remodeling country houses, but if any of them ever
pointed out the mortgage difficulties on such properties, I have
failed to dig it up. This is natural because, as always, they show
the pretty surface while ignoring the shaky substructures.

During this period there was also a general air of irresponsibility
as in this editorial by Margaret Culkin Banning, which said: "You
might as well spend it," the theme of this being: I might as well
spend my money now. Maybe next year I won't have it!

Altogether there was an air of weariness that seeped into almost
everything in the magazines even to such matters as exercise. There
was a piece about taking exercises in bed that would have been
first rate for an older woman or semi-invalid, but these exercises
were suggested for young girls. They were called "Sitting Up In
Bed" and the girls stretched their arms, brought up their knees and
kicked, imitating a baby in a crib. It was a piece of foolishness,
a sign of the desperate search for something to say.

Food coverage was not as good as that in *Good Housekeeping*,
the recipes were not as attractively displayed, the instructions not
as clear. Perhaps the editors felt their own lack of quality because
they made up for this by little flirtations with their readers. Salmon

in a salad "coos with pleasure," but if you add peas to the salad, "it sings right out in meeting." And another, curious in a belt-tightening decade, that preparing delicious food was "an expense item that will make the pocketbook do a tango from sheer exuberance."

But the readers were not responsive. The circulation of *Ladies' Home Journal* kept sliding downward. This of course was true of most of the women's magazines, if not all of them. People didn't have the money to spend. But later events showed that there were special reasons for the *Ladies' Home Journal's* decline, reasons like uncertain editing and inferior service departments.

It was about this time that the various women's magazines reminded themselves of *Sex*. Sex had nearly always been treated by them as something purely romantic; but now times were changing and why should they miss the newsstand allure? Sex could be explosive, but it could sell magazines, as we will show more fully in another chapter.

Today, under its present editorship the *Ladies' Home Journal* has found a formula that may work. Roughly it seems to imitate the pattern of the *Saturday Evening Post,* in a feminized version.

Fundamental is a complete novelette or what they call "novella" in each issue. The *Journal* costs thirty-five cents a copy. You can buy a copy of a paperbound book (certainly easier to read than these complete novelettes) for a quarter. But in addition, the *Ladies' Home Journal* has beautiful pictures, attractive ads, a measure of telling you what you ought to do to improve the world. Reading this makes a woman feel that the world is getting better and that she has had something to do about it.

Another regular feature is a page by Dorothy Thompson. If sometimes Miss Thompson is a little inconsistent, that makes her all the more interesting. What could be more boring than a consistent columnist? Dorothy Thompson is never cute or coy. She is often eager, even passionate, sometimes unreasonable. Her common sense on many subjects is certainly a relief from Mrs. Roosevelt's honey in *McCall's*.

Obviously the editors of the *Journal* are going along on a big name policy. Among the "big names" in 1959 were Daphne duMaurier, Jean Kerr, Phyllis McGinley, Munro Leaf, Walter Lippman, John P. Marquand, Benjamin Spock, Lady Diana Cooper, etc.

The service departments are skimpy except on fashions: [6] There were four articles on fashions. One of these, taking a hint from *Mademoiselle*, is entitled "How To Dress Well on Practically Nothing." Handsomely illustrated, this told the reader that she should buy separate sweaters and skirts, which every female over the age of six knows very well.

Also, with an intention to be funny, are continuing moans about fiendish small children and incompetent mothers. A subject which is by now wearing thin though still an excellent source of income and dinner table talk.

Sometimes, of course, something stimulating comes along as in Phyllis McGinley's piece in the September, 1959, issue. Miss McGinley's thesis is that it's not a good thing for a woman to have a masculine mind, and that women are becoming more and more masculine. To me, there seems little danger, or should I say promise, that women are developing masculine methods of thinking. Instead, in their contest with the male, they are assuming his outward dress, slant and certain techniques. Then it seems to me they mess it all up by thinking in an emotional and feminine fashion.

[6] Some readers may wonder why I have said so little about fashions except here and there at the start of things. I love pretty clothes but feel that I should leave this to more capable hands. I cannot even describe a dress which I have seen just five minutes before.

There are strong indications that the *Ladies' Home Journal* has realized that there is a man in the family and a good deal of the content has been aimed at him. It is done awkwardly and, if I may say so, is a waste of effort. On the whole, the fiction is not of the kind to appeal to men and the material in the special articles a man could find elsewhere. Also, there is the important point that the word "Ladies" may scare a man off, or at least make him feel self-conscious if caught with a copy of the *Ladies' Home Journal*.

On the whole, the 1959 issues strengthen the impression that the *Ladies' Home Journal* is taking inspiration from the *Saturday Evening Post*. The whole effect is handsome, lively, flashy, and rather confusing. It goes to six-and-a-half million women, and as each of these passes hers on, at least, to two others, has a strong influence on about fifteen million women in the country. Nonetheless, because its aims are unsure, it is walking a tight rope.

The most brilliant aspect of the *Ladies' Home Journal* is its self advertising. Seldom has there been a campaign so clever as their "Never Underestimate the Power of a Woman" and why not, since the *Journal* has done so much to build up that power.

7

Follow the Leader

When I went to work for the *Woman's Home Companion* in 1908, I was told to imitate the *Ladies' Home Journal* as closely as possible. Edward Bok had made the *Journal* the bright star in the firmament of the women's magazines. (I seem to have caught an infection. This last sentence seems to have caught Bok's own style.)

The *Companion* had begun as a farm paper in Cleveland in 1873. In 1885 when the *Journal* was already beginning its climb, the *Companion* still looked like a newspaper, small type on newsprint paper, about the size and appearance of a present day tabloid, though not so well illustrated.

Though just as handsome as the *Ladies' Home Journal* in appearance, in 1908 the *Companion* was more small town and back country. Its printing plant and circulation departments were in Springfield, Ohio. I was sent to spend a week there to learn the ropes and to make friends. I found a deep resentment at the takeover by the big city people in New York, which showed up in formal courtesy and invitations to lunch, but not to dinner.

My job was to start a new subscription department, and to develop amateur subscription agents. The magazine already had a large force of professional agents; it also had a Pony Man who enlisted boys with a tantalizing reward of a pony. This was highly successful, as it could never possibly have been in the big city, where people had no place to keep a pony.

Door to door selling of magazines is an arduous business. I was to dress it up in a nice and polite gown, with ruffles. My agents were to be ladies. The word "agent" was never to be used. "Commission" and even "payment" were to be avoided. While the girls were to get just as much for their work as any professional agent, they would get part of it in gifts. Every magazine knows that subscriptions sent in by friendly readers are the most satisfactory. It was this kind of friendly reader who was to be worked on systematically.

The *Ladies' Home Journal* had such a department and it was doing well. They called theirs "The Girls' Club." So we too would have a club. Our girls were to be members of the "Pin Money Club." This talk of "girls" does not mean that we had any age limit for our members. The women's magazine world was full of girls. It was a transition period. The word "ladies" was out of style, and "women" (except in matters like "votes for women") had not come in. The word "woman" in our title was considered a drawback. This was six years before the First World War, which more or less changed ladies to women. Sarah Josepha Hale herself had preferred "woman" to "lady" but, keeeping her readers in mind, she had used the word sparingly. So the women of all ages who worked and mothered (grandmothered too) and sewed and cooked throughout the female world were all girls. They still are, of course.

Each month I was to write a column or two which was to go

in the "book" [1] as editorial matter, intended to attract lady-like readers to become circulation agents. The editors did not like that pose, but they were overruled. After all, you've got to have subscribers to edit for.

In some ways we were able to improve on our *Ladies' Home Journal* model. Later on they improved on our improvements. When we started, their club was impersonal; they had no rules or officers. We had rules, and, our best bet, we had a *Secretary,* for whom we devised the name Margaret Clarke. Oliver Capen, the head of the subscription department, was a cautious man. I found this caution irksome, but he was obviously right, since he became head of several enormous magazines, and I didn't become head of any. There were many conferences about that name—whether it should be Margarite Clarke (two *e* endings) or Margaret Clark (no final *e*'s). We compromised on Margaret Clarke (one final *e*). I was Margaret Clarke, but the picture we used at the head of the column was that of my secretary, a pretty Irish-Italian girl. This was sensible; she took a better photograph than I did. Besides, I would not have been willing to allow my photograph to remain in use, if and when I left the magazine. But my secretary, although she later quit, cheerfully left her photograph behind.

To be a member of the club a girl had to get three subscriptions. For these she got $1.05 in cash and a half-tone reproduction of a photograph of Maude Adams. Although she had not yet played "Peter Pan," she was already the dream girl of America, a dream more ethereal (to say the least) than that called forth by Marilyn Monroe.

We tried a contest for the best workers. I learned then something I have never forgotten, that most women do not like

---

[1] To call a magazine a "book" is considered a sign of illiteracy; yet inside every publication office I've ever known, "the book" is the accepted usage.

contests. There were four prizes, and only four women out of thousands tried to win, and naturally did win. These were the gamblers by temperament. Most of the girls preferred to try for a definite goal, the special honor of belonging to the Inner Circle. Twenty-five subscriptions were the passport to this, and its badge was a small gold brooch, with a diamond chip, designed by Tiffany.

All right, you think these girls were silly. How about Elks? Besides, these members of the Inner Circle got fifteen dollars in cash with their little pins.

Later I started a similar department for *Pictorial Review* and called it "Daughters of the Golden Treasure"; and there the Inner Circle became "Daughters of the Pearl." I also started one for *McCall's*. All these "Clubs" did very well for some years. The "Club" was still running in the *Companion* in 1935 but by then it was only directed to married women for "pin money." Later it disappeared from all the magazines. The present day girl is harder to reach by that sort of bait. She wants a job.

In order to fit in with the kind of writing that was wanted for "the book," I had to modify the vigorous style I had used in writing advertising. Everything had to be softened. I solved the problem by writing all the material in my usual muscular manner and then editing as required. This slight misting of words was not peculiar to my department or to the *Companion*. It was the usual feather-duster style of the women's magazines.

But let me make this clear: in this writing, only the words had to be gentled, not the facts. In later years of advertising women's products, I found that women insist on more facts than men do. It's the language, the approach, that must be softened. Word by word, I sugared my copy and flavored it with vanilla instead of with pepper and salt.

All this sounds pretty cynical, but some of my cynicism wore off as I came to realize the genuine trust these agents gave me. My purely commercial department brought letters asking for advice about intimate, sometimes tragic problems. Some of these women were desperate for someone to talk to, especially those who did not want their friends to know their troubles. I was a stranger. This is a pattern well known to any psychiatrist. To me at that time it was new, and I was moved and astonished. The girls sent presents, too, and invitations to visit.

Every department of a woman's magazine gets such letters. This faith is less now than it used to be, but not much less. A man's magazine seldom calls forth such trust in the omniscience of its editors.

The titular editor-in-chief of the *Woman's Home Companion* was Fred Collins, and the impression in the shop was that he was out of place in a woman's magazine. He was an intelligent, charming man. *Who's Who* says that he left the *Companion* shortly afterward and had a lively career on general magazines and radio. The real editor then and for many years afterward was Gertrude Lane. Miss Lane became editor-in-chief in 1911 and remained so for thirty years. She had come to the magazine in a small job when she was twenty and when she died she was getting $50,000 a year. She was an able woman, cool and quiet on the surface. After she had been in charge for a few years she found her feet on the job and did not need to follow anyone else's pattern. But who doesn't watch his competitors and learn from them?

Her program sounded fine: She said: "In editing the *Woman's Home Companion* I keep constantly in mind a picture of the housewife of today as I see her. She is not the woman who wants to do *more* housework, but the woman who wants to do *less* housework so that she will have more time for other things. She is intelligent and clear headed; I must tell the truth. She is busy, I must not waste her time. She is forever seeking new ideas; I must keep her in touch with the best. Her horizon is ever extending, her interest broadening; the pages of *Woman's Home Companion* must reflect the sanest and most constructive thought on the vital issues of the day."

No doubt she meant some of it. What they printed in the magazine helped women along the democratic road. It taught them manners, it taught them how to make better-looking houses. Mind you, not better homes, not inner culture, but *better-looking* houses, according to the standards of that day, and better manners that lifted a woman's spirits and gave her a step up.

Naturally, the magazine went along with the development of the conception of power for women. All its editors believed in that. It was full of instruction and command, of orders that posed as suggestions. Naturally, too, the woman reader was the most important member of her household, and so carried on the matriarchal idea of Sarah Josepha Hale.

Speech in that office was gentle, voices were low, smiles were sweet. They were as cold-headed a group of people as I've ever known. But don't let's get the wrong idea from all that. Recently, I have been looking over copies of *Woman's Home Companion* for those years. And under all the sugary icing on top, the magazine had toughness. Its contents, which bored me so much at the time, in historical perspective seem to me practical and strong.

Their basic pattern was still the one laid down by Sarah Josepha Hale. Many of the departments established in *Godey's* were still part of the pattern of the *Companion*. There were some new ones, of course. New things had come in. But the tone was the same, that is, the tone of instruction, of sweet command. It was there in every issue and in every article. The magazine was a matriarch.

Preachy departments by Edward Everett Hale (no relation to Sarah Josepha) were tiresome and silly. Others by Anna Steese Richardson were tiresome, but not silly. But the "service" parts of the magazine were solid, though they were, of course, slanted by the advertising. There was still plenty of fresh information to give to women for their home-making and family-raising jobs. The deeply rutted, worn paths that women's magazines have to travel now were then still open roads full of interesting new ways.

The cooking department could not have been better. Its editor was Fannie Merritt Farmer, and if you have recently looked at this great cook's recipes, you realize that Mrs. Farmer knew her stuff. Today there are more amusing and more esoteric cooks, but none with her influence. The desperation which has fallen on cooking departments, because the recipes have all been wrung dry, has driven them to pages of expensive kitchen plans instead of recipes.

Needless to say, there was nothing about reducing diets, that top circulation-puller of recent years. Most women wore corsets and so they didn't have to reduce down to their bones in order not to waggle. Men liked them plump. I think they still do.

There was a brief department of advice for "the girl who earns her own living," at which a modern girl would hoot. Some of the advice is remote, indeed, as, for instance, "You can wear oxford ties to business if it (*sic*) does not endanger your health." For the period in which it appeared, that was sensible. Oxfords were just beginning to replace high shoes, and high shoes gave a better support to the foot. I wish Anna Steese Richardson, who wrote that, could meet the girl I overheard in a shoe store the other day. She was complaining, "But Mother, I don't want those shoes. They have no sex. You want me to wear shoes with no sex?"

You will notice that women still did not "work"—they "went to business." They didn't have jobs; they "accepted positions."

This was a time of extreme excitement about the franchise for women. That was serenely overlooked in the *Companion*. Also blandly ignored were such front page news people as Theodore

Roosevelt and Eugene Debs, and unpleasant catastrophes like the Triangle Fire.

Fiction in the *Ladies' Home Journal* was better, on the whole, but Juliet Wilbur Tompkins wrote some excellent short stories for the *Woman's Home Companion*. The general tone of fiction, however, was dreary with noble men and chaste women in noble and chaste situations, though this was in the time when Edward VII and Lily Langtry were gallivanting around.

For the parents of children there was very little—an occasional article, one headed "Are Babies Moral?" and another, "Disciplining a Crying Baby." Negroes were treated exclusively as subjects of humor.

The *Companion* had about the same standards as all the other big women's magazines of the time, except in two respects. *Good Housekeeping* had more about food, and nearly all the others had better fashion deparments. The fashion department in the *Woman's Home Companion* was really deplorable. I think they knew it, but the fashion editor had been with the magazine a long time; it seems to me that she was a stockholder.

One omission seems odd. Ready-made clothes were very expensive and not of the first fashion. So, during this period, there was a great deal of "making over." There were plenty of "little seamstresses." It seems to me that I was always having Miss Engstrom, my seamstress, making over something or other. Now this would seem to be a natural for the fashion department of the *Woman's Home Companion*. It wasn't mentioned in those issues which I have seen. Perhaps it didn't fit the pretentious pattern of seeming better than you were, of "Keeping up with the Joneses."

Once in a while something popped up in the magazine which has no relation to its general pattern and which stands out like a sore thumb; for instance, this article, "The Lepers of Molokai," by

Jack London. I suppose it was meant to show "broad interests" and of course Jack London was a big name.

Bok's success with his anti-nostrum campaign had put the *Journal* away out in front in the fight for cleaner products for the public. The *Companion* searched for something as good. In 1911, they found it in "The Clean and Dirty Grocery Stores." It was perfect. Every woman could look around her and see the need because most ordinary grocery stores were pretty messy at that time. And who could object to making them clean?

Advertisers were delighted because this was the opening gun in a campaign to promote advertised brands, which were just beginning to learn how to talk. Miss Lane entitled her first article "The Cat in the Cracker Barrel." It brought a flood of advertising into the magazine. The general idea was used by all the women's magazines, in one form or another, but the *Woman's Home Companion* seems to have shown more ability in its handling. *Good Housekeeping* had the more brilliant idea in its "Seal" and went far ahead of the others in food advertising.

Another of Miss Lane's successes was the Better Babies Bureau, which asked editorial advice from readers. This was wishful thinking which paid off. But with these and other devices the magazine rose under Miss Lane from 727,000 to 3,000,000 circulation.

The basic theme of the magazine was "Home and Mother." But among the top editors there was not one who was a mother or who had a husband. Home was strictly a "bachelor girl" affair, sometimes shared with another woman. Today the tendency has changed, with a bias toward married women. With an air of false *bonhomie,* the people at the *Woman's Home Companion* always talked about the "Companion Family." But there was no spirit of democracy in the office at all. From top to bottom the class divisions were distinctly and sharply held. It was even reflected in the attitude of the reception girl who was so top-lofty with visiting authors and illustrators that it was a joke to outsiders. Snobbishness was much less noticeable in advertising agencies in which I worked later than in the *Woman's Home Companion.* This may not have been so on other magazines, except later, at *Vogue,* where it was simply grotesque.

So, for more than a generation the various women's magazines watched each other, and picked up ideas, and manner. They still do. But now there are a number of new patterns, as in *Woman's Day, Mademoiselle* and *Family Circle. Good Housekeeping* also, both in format and content, dug out new paths. But the majority played follow-the-leader and ring-around-the-rosie, relying upon imitations and repetitions, even when it led them toward ruin.

8

Decline and Fall

At the outbreak of the first World War, all the women's magazines had been sure that no one would have money, certainly
not for a luxury like magazines. In this attitude they were at one
with the book publishers, who fully expected to dry on the vine,
because who would read a book during the war?

They were both wrong; the women's magazines came booming
through the war; people bought more books and magazines because they had more money, and because there were new things
to read about, actual experiences in wartime for instance. And because there were fewer men and fewer entertainments. At the end
of the war there was a positive galaxy of prosperous magazines,
bulbous with subscribers and advertising.

The Big Six were *Ladies' Home Journal, Good Housekeeping,
Woman's Home Companion, McCall's, Pictorial Review* and *Delineator*. In contents they were all much alike, though there were
minor differences. *Good Housekeeeping* had more about food and
also pushed its Seal of Approval. *McCall's, Pictorial Review* and
Delineator leaned more heavily to patterns.

Good Housekeeping was a somewhat handier size than the others, as it is today. The rest were galumphing big things, hard to read, but dearly beloved by advertisers, because their large-page size made their products look impressive. This obsession with size has cost many advertisers a good deal of money. But if you're an experienced advertising agent trying to impress your client, you know he falls for the grand spread, with big pictures of his lovely product. Mail order advertisers know better. Also it's much harder work and takes more knowledge to do a good job in smaller space.

The *Ladies' Home Journal* led in advertising and circulation, but the *Companion* came a close second. In content these two issues were typical of the big women's home service magazines of the period.[1]

The *Woman's Home Companion* looked handsome ("good eye appeal"), but the illustrations were not up to what they would be today. Color photography (or photo-journalism) has come a long way since then. Take food. Neither advertiser nor editor knew how to photograph food so that it looked good to eat. Food was shown in drawings, and artists were doing some good still lifes on it, but this was very expensive and time consuming. Now food is photographed in full color at comparatively little expense. In the course of this progress the food itself has suffered some. A lemon meringue pie, to be photogenic, must be stiff, hence full of corn starch. The wobbliness that belongs to a good lemon custard, is now generally considered, even by the consumer, a sign of the second-rate.

In the *Woman's Home Companion,* the sections of practical interest to women were very good. They had comparatively little mush and no chi-chi at all. For expectant mothers there was good

[1] We omit *Vogue* and *Harper's Bazaar* because they do not come under this category.

material from the *Companion's* "Better Babies Bureau," an astute title for an excellent department. The magazine offered circulars showing designs for maternity dresses and common-sense layettes. Women who were "expecting" were still ashamed in 1919. These circulars were sent in a plain envelope with nothing outside to identify the contents, so that the woman was "safe" in receiving them.

The Better Babies' Bureau also gave suggestions for contests and club work. These carried on the "power for women" idea. Like most other club activities promoted by the women's magazines, these had some merit. Their weakness was that they encouraged women to act on matters they didn't bother to study. So they often didn't know what they were talking about. They just took someone's word for it; in this case an editorial board whose interests were entirely commercial. Of course, handing over of judgment did not pass with that period. It still exists.

Nearly all this material, and a lot more on the practical side, the readers could have got for almost nothing from the Government Printing Office. Much of it came right out of these government publications. I, for one, long ago found them of great help in the writing of advertising.

But maybe these editors knew what they were doing. Americans, women especially, seemed to distrust any information disseminated by the government. In 1950, *Woman's Day* with practical sense and honesty, began to list some of the government publications with descriptions. The effort seems to have been a dud. Women readers didn't find the government publications as glamorous as the magazines. They had more faith in the shiny print and gooey talk of their periodicals than they had in the austere-looking government publications, and private advertisers smelled competition. And the printing office did not advertise its own work. Today these publications are sent out by the millions. More women have learned to depend on them.

The *Companion's* advice to parents would make today's mother wish she had been bringing up her child in 1919. The young children there described didn't seem to have any temper tantrums. There was none of this business about "she won't talk" or "she won't eat." Punishment did not give parents a sense of guilt about their own bad tempers. And how fearfully obedient those children were! But they were called "innocents" not "monsters."

Another department that throws light on the attitude of the period is "The Tower Room," a department for girls. One girl wrote, "My father and mother do not understand me." Note that this was a *girl,* not a *teenager.* The department answered, "It is not of great importance whether we are understood, but what is of lasting and permanent importance is that we should understand others."

No fear of frustration here. The editors found this situation perfectly normal, since nearly all teenagers feel misunderstood.

The First World War caused a revolution in the thinking of America and especially of its women. It shortened skirts, bobbed hair, brought freedom for women to smoke in public, introduced the after-dinner highball at home in the United States. None of this, however, was shown or discussed in the 1919 women's magazines, except the shortening of skirts and hair. The rest was obviously still considered dangerous ground.

But often what they wouldn't say in articles or editorials, they would get across in fiction. Much of the fiction was squeamish and snobbish. The heroes were from "the right people"; the heroines from "the best people." They had the noblest ideals. But that was just the wrapper on the goods. Underneath, the heroines were women of much rough and varied experience in both love and life, hard as nails, and willing to break any rule to obtain whatever pure and noble ideal they were pursuing. They were experienced women who had somehow managed to creep into the pure and beautiful bodies of eighteen-year-old girls.

It was a popular formula for all the women's magazines, including the *Woman's Home Companion*. And it was as close as the magazines could come to approving openly the new freedom for women.

There was a self-help department with suggestions of this sort: "How to Make Soap from Inedible Fats." This was due to the war shortage of soap. And some older-bodied ladies did make their own soap . . . awful stuff but very cleansing.

The fashion and pattern departments were both excellent, though the descriptions were pretentious, as "American girl depends on her ally *Le Tailleur* in all her clothing emergencies." Refreshing is a group of patterns for "stout young girls"; franker than today's nonsense of "chubby sub-teens."

The food department was good too. Women were still sifting flour and creaming shortening. No ready-to-cook products, frozen or unfrozen. (Did they taste better, or was I just younger?) A department the *Companion* called "Miss Farmer's School of Cookery" gave some itemized costs for a cake to make at home and sell. A loaf of chocolate marshmallow cake, seven inches square, cost forty-two and one-half cents to make. It would cost about a dollar and a half today. All the recipes seem to have been based on the idea that the women knew how to cook. They had no oven thermometers.

One issue of the *Companion* introduced a new kitchen. It had a large window, a dumb waiter to bring food from the basement, an ice-box with one door facing outside so that the iceman didn't have to come into the house. This may seem a trivial detail to a housekeeper of the 1960's, but I assure you that that outside ice door seemed wonderful to us at the time. It meant that no one had to stay home to wait for the iceman. As today a woman says, "I can't come because I haven't a baby-sitter," in 1919 she would say, "I can't come because I have to wait for the iceman." That gave rise to the endless jokes about the iceman, who actually seldom looked the part of a Don Juan. No wonder Eugene O'Neill wrote a grim play about him.

The *Companion* also advised about preparing yourself for entering the business world; the Vice-President of the Bush Terminal Railroad says that "in the first position for any girl the salary should be given little or no consideration but every care should be taken to get placed in the right surroundings."

The subject of winning a husband and keeping him was handled delicately under the head, "Before and After Marriage." The *Companion* did not speak out directly to the reader, but used the fictional medium of a nearly engaged girl talking to a married girl friend. These are the qualifications the girl on the hunt demanded of her hoped-for husband: "idealism in attitude toward life and brilliance of intellect," otherwise he would bore her; she could put up with "temperamental irritability and bossiness and a certain amount of conceit *but* she despised stinginess or smallness in any form."

In 1919 the *Companion* was still a home-body magazine, with good practical sense, but also with the flattery, the invitations to power, the soft-soap and the soft talk characteristic of the breed. Part of the soft talk was a dreadful coyness, as in a picture story of a blonde facing a brunette: "Aha, we fooled you! Dorothy Gish is wearing a wig here and oh, so effectively!"

In 1919 the influence of Edward Bok was still very strong. He had just retired as editor of the *Ladies' Home Journal*. But by 1935, four years before the Second World War, his influence had waned. Miss Lane, also an able editor, retired in 1940. The era of the big fumble was already strong in the women's magazines. I have said elsewhere that successful editors were those who published what they themselves liked; that when an editor kept thinking would the public like this or that, and when he disregarded his own tastes, the result was a milk-and-water affair. Editors like Mrs. Hale, Bok, Mencken, Harold Ross—their standards were their own.

The practical departments were the stand-bys, the real strength of the women's magazines. By 1935 these departments had weakened. Food became pretty fancy. For two generations all of the magazines had been publishing recipes. For years they had had something new to say, good guidance to the home cook. But how many times can you run the same piece? How many times can you tell the cook that she should brown her chunks of meat before she sets them to simmer with vegetables for the stew? How many times can you tell her to dip the peaches and tomatoes in boiling water to make them easy to peel? (She knew it anyhow). They had to find something else.

So now it was gourmet cookery. Chicken in white wine, very good too. But why describe spaghetti sauce thus: "There's a delicacy to do honor to a steaming plate of spaghetti." The familiar baking dish becomes the "obliging casserole" . . . it cooks a hearty dinner and gives you time to "gossip with your family." There was a sensible article on how to buy meat cuts. The same thing had appeared in old cook books, and in government bulletins. Still, maybe in 1935 women didn't know about it.

Babies—the *Companion* still kept its eye on them. Advice to "Expectant Mothers" came out into the open and with frills. No more plain envelope so that mother could "feel safe." But no direct talk—just the same old imitation "Club" and "Circle" we had in 1908. There was an Expectant Mothers' Circle for information on prenatal care . . . fifty cents. The Nursery Club was for mothers of small babies, and another Nursery Club for mothers with babies from one to five. All the information was sensible but the editors felt the need to trick it up. Were the replies getting fewer?

Obviously the editors were thinking that women of today are interested in a lot of things; let's see what we can find that maybe they'd like to read. Let's have something about those people on relief; they don't buy the magazine, but people do talk about them, so James Truslow Adams, historian, had a piece showing that most people on relief have no sense of inferiority or personal fault. The Brownings contributed some new letter (everybody's talking about that play, *The Barretts of Wimpole Street,* of course) and how about a contract bridge quiz?

These articles had one basic idea, then and now. "Let's give them something to talk about when they go out to dinner or when they go to the club." Not something to *know* but something to *talk* about. There was a faint sense of confusion, a lack of focus, a lack of solidity.

By 1950, all the tendencies shown in 1935 came to fruition. The service departments were less solid. Inevitably, the new recipes featured ready-made food, mixes, gravies, sauces, syrups, anything in a bottle or jar or box. Some of these were good, the cake mixes for instance. Many of the dishes were tasteless when "instantly cooked." But who cares? There's more time—more time for hobbies and community work.

A piece about choosing an electric washer may be sensible enough, but was there any mention of washers that didn't advertise in the *Companion?* Lots more space for fashions with emphasis on ready-made clothes. Sewing tricks, how to make ripping easy.

Lots about beauty. The *"Companion* Way to Makeup Magic."

"Find out the type you are (if you plan on being shy, bold, or otherwise)." Different makeups for different times of day, different places, and the effects the lighting will have on makeup.

Here I want to say something about the beauty-swooning goo in all these magazines. Many young women wonder what their grandmothers used to do. Did they just perspire and look dowdy? Well, for perspiration they used baking soda; for face masks they used white of egg, for rough hands they used glycerine and rose water. All of them were cheap and as effective as many of the fanciest packages with exquisite labels and come-hither names. But who would advertise the white of an egg? Or a ten-cent package of baking soda when there was a dollar cream? When I was lecturing to a college group, I found that the youngsters all knew that many five-and-ten-cent store cosmetics were as good as expensive ones wrapped up la-la, some better. But they did not look as swanky on a dressing table. A three-dollar jar of face cream costs about seven cents to make, package included. Is it possible the beauty editors didn't know this? Sure they did. But where was the profit in saying so. A magazine has to live.

In the children's section, just one article—wouldn't you know? "When Your Children Ask About Sex."

In the fiction, the "other man" and the "other woman" are as busy as bees, as birds and bees in fact. Happiness meant someone you were not married to. The stories had arrived a little late on this subject. The twenties were the years that were biggest for changing around to new pastures among the elite.

In the search for something the reader might like there was more "humor," some bright, some unfunny. One really funny quote from Jerome K. Jerome—"I like work. It fascinates me. I can look at it for hours."

But on the whole there was purpose and gravity, with the underlying motif, as always, more power to women. It was pretentious, though. There was a Department of Human Relations, and a Good Citizenship Bureau in one issue of the *Companion*. Its tone: Who runs your community? (The drawing for this article showed the women's clubs using a broom to sweep out gangsters, racketeers, criminals.) For six cents in stamps, the *Woman's Home Companion* would send a copy of the program called "The Crusade on Crime."

The build-up of women's power had become standardized, everything in a package which the *magazine* would send you, and which dealt with vital community problems. All thinking was done for you since the package included speeches, plans of action, guest speakers. (What a chance for propaganda . . . and how they used that chance! But every bit of the material was shallow; none of it went to the root of the subject.)

Naturally, the *Companion* wanted women to be happy; it had a Six Day Program for that. The general nature of its cure for the blues:

One day: Go calling. Make two brief calls, one on an old friend, the other on some one you haven't seen in a long time.

Another day: Make a firm date to go shopping with a friend the day after tomorrow.

Still another day: You've been meaning to invite that couple to dinner for months. Call them this P.M. and make a date for sometime next month.

Only an editor fishing desperately for something to say could think up anything like that. Result: the *Woman's Home Companion* folded in 1958. There had been a confusion of management at the top. Editors were changed with dizzying speed. Prices of production were too high.

But there was more than that to the collapse. *Pictorial Review* and *Delineator* had already gone out of business, *McCall's* and *Ladies' Home Journal* were worried. Only *Good Housekeeping* seemed to be solid. The truth is that all of them had lost touch with their women; the old format no longer had any place. In its issue of July 9, 1958, *Time* said, "*Woman's Home Companion* (circulation 4,117,734), which was making a profit until 1953, has lost more than $1,000,000 in advertising in the last six months."

A glance at the issue of July, 1956, tells one reason why this once sturdy magazine went into the doldrums. It is flabby, pointless. It strains for sensational effects. The solid information that a woman might need is almost entirely lacking. It was edited with a desperate "What will they like?" instead of "What do I like?"

Gossip said that the continued bumbling and interference of the owners was the cause of some of this editorial confusion. The editors began to take a do-nothing and-you-will-do-no-wrong attitude. The gossip among the insiders began to filter out into the trade. Talkative employees remarked here and there that the magazine was about to be sold. At this news, advertisers began to withdraw their accounts, and that meant the end.

When the *Woman's Home Companion* went out of business it was a shock to the others in the magazine world. The circulation of the magazine was over four million of which two hundred thousand subscribers had been recently acquired. Much of this increased circulation, however, had been acquired at much too high a price. Readers secured through either high-pressure salesmanship or virtual give-aways do not value a publication and sometimes do not even bother to look at it.

But there were other reasons for the *Woman's Home Companion's* troubles. These were fundamental ones and applied to all the "big" women's magazines. There were simply too many such magazines of a general nature (there still are) in an age of specialization. Also there were television and radio, enemies to the magazines because they were both distractors from reading and users of the advertisers' money. The newspapers were beginning to use color advertisements, which had been one of the major advantages of the magazines over the newspapers. Another enemy to the women's magazines is the low-priced reprint or paperback. Many women who bought the magazines for fiction, now pick up a paperbound book. This applies especially to women who read on the way to work, when a big magazine is a nuisance.

But in the end, it is the contents of a magazine which determines its fate; and some of the general women's magazines have been offering too little for too long. But, like trees, it is surprising how much abuse they will stand before they fall.[2]

[2] After the *Woman's Home Companion* folded, the Crowell-Collier Publishing Co. which owned it, bought into The Macmillan Co., book publishers, and its affairs passed from the red into the black, with estimated earnings for the first quarter of 1960 up about 40 percent.

9 ❦

The Seal of Approval

Customs march on and consciences move,
But what do the *Seals of Approval* approve?
—C. M.

In the latter part of the nineteenth century a number of new
women's magazines had been born. *McCall's* was founded in 1870,
Woman's Home Companion in 1873, *Good Housekeeping* in
1885. Most of them started in a small, simple way, some with
farm women in mind, some intended for small towns. There
wasn't much for the big city woman.

Godey's Lady's Book was edited for the upper classes, and it had
a big city point of view. But by 1890, Mrs. Hale and Godey
were both dead, and *Godey's* had petered out. Nevertheless, the
newer magazines all followed the pattern Mrs. Hale had set forth,
a mélange of amusement, instruction, and service. The tone was,
like hers, a mixture of flattery and command. But they went along
on this pattern vaguely, with no real understanding of their public.

Bok had changed all that. He had shot adrenalin into the
women's magazines, and through them, into the women's world.
He had aimed directly at the middle-class woman, and he knew her

well. After Bok had established the *Ladies' Home Journal* as the leader in circulation, advertising and influence, all the others began to imitate him. In the *Woman's Home Companion* the imitation was careful and deliberate. *Good Housekeeping,* however, used more originality. It gave much more space to food. That was wise, because good times or bad, people have to eat. *Good House-keeping* has turned out to be the most consistent money-maker of the lot. But that success wasn't due just to emphasis on food. Particularly it was due to a sales idea and one man. The idea was the Good Housekeeping Seal of Approval. The man was Dr. Harvey A. Wiley, the greatest fighter for purity in foods and medicines that this country has ever seen. As for the Seal I don't know any advertising gimmick with such a long-lasting solid success. All over America and anywhere in the world where our people have gone, women demand the Good Housekeeping Seal of Approval on their purchases. They feel an almost religious faith in its magic.

When a man named Clark W. Bryan started *Good House-keeping* in 1885, he sent it forth from Holyoke, Massachusetts, with these resounding words, "In the interests of the higher life of the household and to perpetuate perfection." In spite of these ideals, the magazine didn't really amount to much until William Randolph Hearst bought it about 1912. The company which owned it in 1901 had tried to pioneer a bit, without disturbing its imitation of the *Ladies' Home Journal*, by establishing something called the Good Housekeeping Institute. This Institute was supposed to give readers information about advertised products. The Institute was a poor thing, but it interested advertisers.

William Randolph Hearst was not one to go along on someone else's pattern. When he took over the magazine in 1912, things began to happen to its colorless pages. He threw the limelight on its food pages. At that time there was one man in the United

States who stood out above the rest in the matter of food. Everyone who read a newspaper knew about Harvey A. Wiley, M.D. Everyone knew how he had fought for clean, pure foods and against fraudulent drugs.

Until the Civil War most of the people in this country grew their own food or bought it from people they knew well. There was little preserving done except in home canning, salting and smoking. Some foods were canned commercially, but the business was small. After the Civil War the whole nature of the country changed and with this change came the preserving of food on a commercial basis. With neither conscience nor supervision, food processors with complete abandon shoveled dirt into the sugar and flour, spooned germs into the milk and scattered the poison of spoiled tomatoes. Foreigners couldn't do this to our people. There was a law forbidding the importation of adulterated foods, but this did not apply to the native packers, who profited greatly from import restrictions.

That's how things stood when Dr. Harvey A. Wiley came to Washington. Wiley came from Indiana, was brought up in a household where intelligence was combined with a narrow religious code. He developed a passion for chemistry, graduated from Harvard, then went to the University of Berlin where he learned the importance of close examination of food products. He returned to head the Chemistry Department at Purdue University. There his real career began, in 1878. Twenty-five intensive, relentless years were to pass before his work began to have any effect.

Finally he became Chemist for the Department of Agriculture in Washington. He had little to work with in his new office. There was not even any apparatus with which to make his tests on foods. He got the necessary equipment at last, but after he published his reports on the bad conditions he had found, higher-ups promptly shut him up. He went on with his work, waiting patiently for a chance to get word to the public about what it was eating. He didn't stand alone in his fight. Several of the states had passed laws to ensure purity in foods. Senators and Representatives from these states naturally worked along with Wiley, especially since the pure food states could not stop shipments of spoiled food in interstate trade. On the other hand, manufacturers, processors and advertisers were pounding away at him with considerable enthusiasm and a lot of money.

Dr. Wiley could not reach the public with his information until 1902, when he got a sensational publicity idea. He organized a group of twelve healthy young men and for five years fed them small doses of the then current food preservatives. It may seem like a ruthless idea, and it is true that Dr. Wiley, when fighting for pure foods, did not always use pure methods. The publicity idea caught on with the newspapers which at once called the group "The Poison Squad." He was able at last to show the country the bad effects of even the small dosage he was using. The public finally caught on and was indignant at what it was putting into its stomach.

Some newspapers and magazines began to fight for Wiley and to clean bad food out of their advertising pages. All this worked into a head of steam until finally, in 1906, Congress passed Dr. Wiley's Pure Food and Drug Act.

The food processors and manufacturers got busy with propaganda and court procedures. They called Wiley a crank which, thank goodness, he was. They worked up false scandals about him; got him charged with overpaying one of his people out of public funds. For a while they won. By an old political device, President Theodore Roosevelt appointed a board to enforce the law and that board quietly reversed all Wiley's decisions. But the public refused to lie down and say uncle, and a number of processors began to toe the line. (Of course there had always been some honest and clean manufacturers.) The charges and the resultant investigation backfired when President Taft and Congress stood by Wiley. It was a sensational victory. But Wiley thought there were too many road blocks against him in government service. In 1912 he resigned from the Bureau of Chemistry and was immediately deluged with gold-lined offers from food manufacturers and others. In his autobiography he says that "one very reliable company" offered him $125,000 a year, a fabulous sum for that day. The company was pledged to deal only in unadulterated whiskey, gin and rum.

The offer with the smallest salary, he says, came from *Good Housekeeping*. But the freedom of expression *Good Housekeeping* offered was so complete that he signed at once to become contributing editor and Director of the Good Housekeeping Bureau of Foods, Sanitation and Health. That was in 1912 and he worked with the magazine until 1929. He pays the organization a high compliment when he says that throughout he had "steadily preached the doctrine of child welfare, health, and proper diet." And an even higher compliment when he adds, "A great deal of my work has been censoring of advertising. One would think that businessmen wishing to make the magazine financially remunerative would have objected to the rejection of the many articles that came under my ban. However, *Good Housekeeping* has never advertised any articles that came under my censorship, unless approved by me. In seventeen years more than a million dollars of advertising offered *Good Housekeeping* in my department has been rejected."

The language may be stuffy, but the intention was first-rate. A lawyer might quibble over the words "that came under my censorship" as leaving a loophole, but I doubt if Wiley meant it that way.

Dr. Wiley became head of the Good Housekeeping Institute in 1912. Its Seal of Approval indicated that the magazine had passed a product with an A-plus. In the issue of June, 1919, *Good House-keeping* explained its Seal of Approval in this brief and forthright manner:

Good Housekeeping guarantees its advertisements. *Good Housekeeping* maintains laboratories where all food products are tested and all household appliances are tried out before they are admitted to our advertising pages. *Good Housekeeping* will not accept the advertisement of any kind of a product in which it does not have full confidence. *Good Housekeeping* will not knowingly advertise a good product for a wrong purpose.

Forty years later, *Good Housekeeping* had found some booby traps in the above guarantee and was much more cautious. Here is the longer and more evasive guarantee of 1959:

If any guaranteed product or service is not as advertised herein, it will, upon request and verification of complaint, be replaced, or the money paid therefor refunded.

Good Housekeeping satisfies itself that products and services advertised in the magazine are good products or services. Certain advertising claims such as those of taste and odor, are purely subjective, and unless patently erroneous, are accepted and guaranteed even if not the opinion of *Good Housekeeping*. Some products presuppose proper installation and/or servicing and neither the manufacturer nor *Good Housekeeping* can be responsible for such work done by dealers or independent contractors. Insurance, real estate and institutional advertisements cannot be guaranteed.

Since 1941 the magazine itself did not use the words "seal of approval," although its advertisers did. *Good Housekeeping* informs me that since that date the magazine uses the words "consumer's guarantee" and "guarantee seal."

If we examine this carefully, we see that its cautious conditions are milder than they appear at first glance. But in the beginning it was the most remarkable shot in the arm ever received by an American magazine.

I was in the advertising business when the Seal of Approval was introduced. When we heard the news an icy chill ran down the agency backbone. Advertisers thought and said "Now, we're in for it." Dr. Wiley had a reputation as a fanatic (crank, we called him). However, we had no drug advertising and the various products we did handle did not come under his ban. Other agencies with more questionable accounts went into a tailspin. Under the Federal laws, many products which flourished locally could no longer be sold in interstate commerce.

But many years have passed since that noble experiment and now it turned out *Good Housekeeping* does not have a thing to worry about, because advertisers say that they can usually get the Seal of Approval by placing a certain amount of advertising in the magazine, as indicated clearly in the following extract:

Three magazines particularly have accentuated this possibly naive public faith by granting advertisers a specific recommendation in return for a certain minimum advertising schedule. The Good Housekeeping Seal of Approval, the Parents' Magazine Commendation Seal, and the American Medical Association Journal Seal of Acceptance. In all these three cases some testing of the product is performed by a special section of the magazine staff to determine that it will not actually harm people who buy it (there is a possible legal liability in these situations if the new blood-iron remedy, for example, turns out to be poisonous). Other magazines simply give away a kind of recommendation as one of the benefits an advertiser buys for his money: The *Saturday Evening Post* will supply tags announcing "A *Post* Recognized Value," which means that there doesn't seem to be anything much wrong with the product as far as a space salesman can tell by looking at it." [1]

As a psychological result of the Seal of Approval campaign, the reputable magazines all gained increased confidence from their

[1] From *Madison Avenue U. S. A.* by Martin Mayer, Harper, 1958.

readers. Also, they all did some cleaning up of their own advertising. In spite of this, and although every other magazine knew how much *Good Housekeeping* had gained from its Seal, still no other, except *Parents' Magazine* and later *McCall's,* adopted any such device.

Two of Wiley's great fights he lost. He was enthusiastic in his hatred of tobacco and adulterated liquor. "The little white slaver" is what he called tobacco and he said: "Tobacco and the potato belong to the same family of plants. They represent the white sheep and the black sheep of the family. . . . Tobacco, one of the most poisonous members of its family, a close relation of the deadly nightshade." The magazine has never carried ads for either.

Nicotine, he said, was "next to prussic acid, the quickest and most deadly poison known." "Employ no person who smokes cigarettes ("Deadly little pills," he called them), from them degeneration is permanent." All this he said in *Good Housekeeping* and he quoted Henry Ford, who went right along with him in the magazine: "If you study the history of any criminal you will find that he is an inveterate smoker."

Wiley was here, as always, sure of himself. He says of diabetes: "There is no remedy, but one may so order his diet and his method of life as to live many years in comparative comfort." It could hardly be expected that he would look into the future and learn about insulin.[2] He believed absolutely that food could be used as a healer and invented a word for it called "Bromotherapy."

Dr. Wiley ran a regular department in which he answered questions on food, sanitation and health. He also wrote a number of articles, sometimes cranky, but usually public-spirited and far ahead of his time. One of these, "Sentinels of Health," pointed up the

[2] He is still right. Insulin is not a remedy; it enables a diabetic, who orders his diet and his life, to live many years in comparative comfort.

danger of disease that crept in through our ports, brought in both by passengers and freight. His methods of protection were excellent, but I wonder how he'd have stopped their entry by plane.

Advertisers, when they could, took advantage fully of his campaigns, but more especially of the Seal of Approval. In a 1959 issue of *Good Housekeeping,* Unguentine carried the Seal of Approval. Unguentine is a good product, but the ad claims: "Two times the pain-relieving medication for faster pain relief." How, I'd like to know, does Unguentine or *Good Housekeeping* so accurately figure the "two times faster" than other pain relievers? But when you read the *Good Housekeeping* guarantee, you see that it leaves a big hole where such statements can drop right in.

Advertisers also use the Good Housekeeping Seal of Approval when pushing their products in other magazines. In the *Ladies' Home Journal* for August, 1959, there was a patent medicine advertisement which read:

Now . . . a special laxative for women. Gives gentle relief more naturally than any ordinary laxative. "During pregnancy and after my baby's birth," wrote a Mrs. Kelly, "I needed a gentle laxative in the nursery." Do try Correctal soon.

Just what part of this announcement does *Good Housekeeping* guarantee? As for *Ladies' Home Journal,* in which this ad ran, we'd like to ask what happened to Bok's vigorous anti-patent medicine campaign? Is the answer to both questions that the tablets are *tiny* and *pink?*

I confess I don't understand how any woman can be silly enough to fall for such talk, but the silliness of women is not the subject of this book—or is it?

In short, during the years between 1912 and 1959, I find the attitude of *Good Housekeeping* itself and of the advertising business toward it, just about the same. I have told how, in 1919, when

I was what was called an account executive, I had no difficulty in getting free publicity for my clients—the women's magazines. The editor usually found the item "of service to her readers."

Here is one example, from *Good Housekeeping*, 1919, of how this was worked (not of my doing). An article on "How The Institute Tests an Electric Range" in the course of which *Good Housekeeping* states: "After reading this article, you may ask yourself 'I wonder how much the manufacturers pay for these thorough searching tests . . . the answer would be 'Not a single penny.'" The point about this is that it is immediately followed by a free offer of recipes to be used with this electric range.

In this general period you will find many news items about Quaker Lace Curtains and ginghams as style items. These I handed out. They were small advertisers, and not bad for the reader but still disguised advertising.

U.S. News and World Report, in its August 10, 1959, issue had this enlightening comment:

Guarantees. The Federal Trade Commission has been campaigning against what it considers misleading representations of guarantees that some manufacturers offer on their products, but an official makes this point: It's still up to the customer to pay attention to what the guarantee says. Many guarantees provide for a diminishing refund or credit over the periods they cover . . . not for a full refund or replacement with a brand-new item. Such guarantees are entirely legal. All the F.T.C. can do is to require that manufacturers make it clear in their advertising when guarantees are limited.

In 1919 as always, before and since, *Good Housekeeping* gave much more space to food than any of the other magazines. Some of this was extremely good and some of it silly. Pictorially the food was more appealing than that in other magazines. The recipes in 1919 began to be concerned with a new worry, that of overweight.

Cleverly *Good Housekeeping* included the number of calories and the protein content in each recipe.

But already in 1919 the advertising had taken a turn which has become all too familiar. "Ninety-seven out of one hundred women reduced on Dietene. Try Dietene just one week. If your overweight is a result of overeating, we guarantee you will lose from one to three pounds per week."

Another modern tendency showed up in 1919 with a series on labor-saving meals. In one sample, which took an hour and a half to prepare, *Good Housekeeping* showed a method by which it could be prepared in only thirty-five minutes. Today's frozen-food cook might be shocked at having to spend thirty-five minutes in preparing a meal.

Good Housekeeping found a successful formula which they have followed right through until today—that is, the step-by-step method of preparation which listed the raw ingredients, the utensils to be used, and last the completed meal. They also plugged a *Good Housekeeping Cook Book* which is very good. Neither the recipes nor the instructions could produce anything but a good dish, if carefully followed. All of this was not only sensible but labor-saving and economical, the reverse of the show-off extravagance common in cookery recipes today.

Of course there was silly and useless material. "In Defense of the Hot Dog" stated that "everybody with common sense knows a hot dog has no social pretensions . . . (but) . . . hot dogs can be made into patricians." In spite of such nonsense, the recipes showed and still show common sense, appealing for the taste of food and its nourishing qualities.

In 1919, *Good Housekeeping's* department on child health was run by Dr. Emmett Holt, Jr. and much of it was very good. You couldn't blame Dr. Holt for not knowing as much as Dr. Spock does today.

A minor criticism might be that there still is too much about baby rashes. There are doctors today who say that sometimes the modern mother, in the cause of sanitation, has gone to the other side of the fence and pictured "germs" as four-headed monsters ready to gobble up babies. So they constantly wash babies, too much and too often, thus removing the natural oils which protect the babies from rashes.

In the do-good campaigns *Good Housekeeping* has seldom in the past followed Bok's pattern. On the whole they have kept hands off. However, Wade H. Nichols, at this writing Editor of *Good Housekeeping*, states in a letter to the author, dated 1960, "Within the past year or so *Good Housekeeping* has covered more current, urgent sensitive and unanswered questions, especially those related to products and false advertising, than has any other magazine in the same period." The word "more" here is challenging. *More* rather than *better?* I think this change in editorial policy is unfortunate; it is along the lines which have done the women's magazines no good and which have led women to sleazy thinking. They stuck to that which was practical help. In fiction and in general articles, *Good Housekeeping* seems less sensational. Also its captions are stronger and less feather-dusting than those in the other magazines.

On the subject of sex, *Good Housekeeping* has been more restrained than the others, but in one of its departments *Good Housekeeping* was typical of the mental attitude in all women's magazines. Once a month the magazine ran a column on what the intelligent woman "May Want to Read, Hear, See and Talk About." "Talk About" are the key words. This is not information or knowledge the reader is seeking for its own sake, it is the usual smattering of tidbits to be used at the dinner table so that a woman may *seem* to be well informed.

Humor was sometimes painful, as in this jargon: "Men is knowledgeous but women is de most undiskivered nation of people whut dere is . . ." If the intended humor was sometimes painful, things which didn't mean to be funny often were: "Decorum for Dogs"— "Getting your dog into Blanche Saunders' School for Training Dogs, is comparable to getting your son into Harvard."

It is evident that from the beginning *Good Housekeeping* has stuck closely to the main function of a woman's magazine—definite information that can be of use. In the issue of July, 1959, there are forty such items, some far-fetched, but most of them sensible. The fiction is poor and obsessed with the lives of movie stars, as you might expect, but the service departments dominate the magazine.

While *Vogue* and *Harper's Bazaar* were for generations leaders in fashions, during the twenties and thirties *Good Housekeeping* was far ahead of its rivals in both the beauty and the sense of its fashion news. In this connection, it is interesting to note that *Good Housekeeping* has held up better than any other of the "big six" magazines. I have saved for last one more possible reason for this. Or perhaps it is merely coincidental that on do's and don't's in the political field *Good Housekeeping* has been most restrained.

10 ∬

More Guarantees of Approval

From the evidence in this and preceding chapters, it appears that the advertising people were in a more advantageous position than the editors of the women's magazines. Since they were anonymous, they could also be less scrupulous. They were also bolder and more original. At this distance in time, it is difficult to determine who thought of the guarantee first; but its chief results were twofold, to get more advertising for the magazines and to sell more goods to the reader. All the women's magazines eventually benefited by Dr. Wiley's early efforts. The advertising business also gained, because, when you get right down to it, the net effect of the Good Housekeeping Bureau, etc., was to train the public to be "loyal" to the advertised products, to take the advertiser's word for it. A special beneficiary of this blind "loyalty" was *McCall's Magazine*.

Good Housekeeping, Ladies' Home Journal and *McCall's* have been known as the "Big Three" because of huge circulation and influence. This was in the 1950's.[1] The "Big Six" of the 1920's had shrunk to three.

[1] In early 1960 *Good Housekeeping* changed and became much more showy and more like its competitors.

There was something in starting a popular pattern business in the nineteenth century which seemed to appeal to a man-and-wife combination. As Mr. and Mrs. Butterick started their business, a little later Mr. James McCall and his wife began another. In 1869, James McCall, a Scotsman, represented a British company which designed dressmaking patterns. These, however, at first were higher grade and more expensive than the Buttericks' patterns, but they developed along the same line. The McCalls felt they needed some kind of catalogue. In 1873 they began to issue one. *The Queen* was made up of four large pages, printed on pink paper. It had very little type, but many woodcuts of patterns. *The Queen* designs were supposed to be better than other patterns because they did not make allowances for seams but expected the dressmaker to use her own judgment. This is puzzling since such a procedure could easily ruin the shape of the garment. *The Queen* developed into a monthly magazine, excepting the two summer months. In the early 1890's the name was changed to *The Queen of Fashion*. Evidently they found it necessary to keep this pretentious title because the magazine was pretty cheap in price and quality.

The name was changed to *McCall's Magazine* in 1897 and that name remained although editors and even owners kept changing. From that time on the magazine began a long career of imitating the *Ladies' Home Journal*. By 1908 its circulation had reached a million. For years after that the magazine stuttered and stumbled along. Its subscription price was fifty cents a year.

Otis Lee Wiese became editor in 1928 and he made a number of experiments. Some of them sounded revolutionary, but they all came to the same in the end. For instance, in 1940, the magazine started a "National Defense" section. It was supposed to do its share in the Second World War. There was a Bureau in Washington to send in hot news. It didn't really accomplish anything, except perhaps provide an air of patriotic endeavor.

In 1949 the magazine began to use Eleanor Roosevelt as a regular contributor. Readers could write in to her personally and ask questions. Her answers to a certain number of them would appear monthly near the front of the magazine. The answers have not been at all startling, but this department brought *McCall's* both publicity and circulation.

In the 1950's *McCall's,* though it looked prosperous and handsome, was declining in circulation and advertising. A new idea was necessary, according to James Playsted Wood.

Prompted perhaps by the success of the so-called "shelter magazines" like *Better Homes and Gardens* it (*McCall's*) announced that it would no longer look upon itself simply as a woman's service magazine, but that it would devote itself to the American woman and her family, becoming a publication for the entire household. Advertisements at the time stated that the new *McCall's* melody would be "togetherness." In appearance and content *McCall's* still looks very much a woman's magazine.

There was a feeling in *McCall's* that the magazine must somehow reach the man of the family. Dad, who had been so cavalierly banished from the women's magazines, was about to be welcomed home again. From this time on the magazine was no longer to appeal to the mother or to the father, but to both as one person.

It is doubtful whether this really brought Dad home or even brought him and Mom any closer to each other. But there is no question at all that the catchword brought attention to *McCall's,* much of this in the form of jokes. Jokes ordinarily are an asset in the publicity and advertising worlds. Henry Ford found out long ago that one of the best publicity gadgets in the world was the circulation of jokes about your product or your advertising.

But if the jokes about "Togetherness" brought attention to *McCall's,* women did not hurry to buy *McCall's,* and men remained absolutely cold to the invitation extended to them. If the editors of the magazine had taken the trouble to examine the history of the women's magazines they might never have made such an absurd and unrealistic attempt to promote what is actually an idealistic concept. In 1900 Arthur T. Vance, editor of the *Woman's Home Companion,* announced that he was going to edit the magazine, *not for women only, but for all members of the family.* "Every month," he wrote, "we will print some story or article aimed at the man of the house." It was a failure, and the effort was soon abandoned.

As *McCall's* continued to pour out material in the "Togetherness" campaign, it also began to lean heavily on sex, marriage and complete novels.

McCall's was generous in the use of space for articles on beauty. There was a great deal about hair-dos and a heavy dependence on weight reduction for filler material. A sample, from September, 1957, was "I Dieted in Secret." This was the heart-warming story of a girl who went from 211 pounds, which would be a size forty-six, down to size twelve, and never even told her husband that she was dieting. A miracle indeed.

Gossip says that *McCall's* was able to go on however, because the corporation which owned it, also published *Redbook. Redbook* was a big money-maker and was basically intended for both men and women. It carried no practical departments. The corporation also owned a huge printing business whose profits helped carry *McCall's.* In spite of all this, things didn't look good.

Suddenly in 1958 came the announcement that the magazine was to have a new editor. He was Herbert R. Mayes, who had just resigned as editor of *Good Housekeeping.* He had been with that magazine for thirty-three years, and had ample experience of the wonder-working magic of the Seal of Approval. On *McCall's* Mr. Mayes found a sister policy called "use tested," which the magazine explains as follows:

If you're like most people, you undoubtedly take a manufacturer's reputation as your asurrance of a product's quality when you buy. But when it comes to the kind of wear and tear it will actually get in your home, it's good to know the product has been Use-Tested by *McCall's*. *McCall's* editors and technicians test all kinds of products under conditions equivalent to home use. And with *McCall's* Use-Tested symbol, they tell you in easy-to-understand, non-technical language, how the product should perform for you and your family in your day-to-day living.

Manufacturers of appliances, home furnishings and almost any packaged product sold in super-markets, drug stores, and department stores can find out how their products can qualify for *McCall's* Use-Tested program by writing to *McCall's*.

Thus apparently *McCall's* went a step further than *Good Housekeeping* since *McCall's* based its guarantee not only on the product when bought, but on tests of how well the product would wear.

On seeing this guarantee, some advertisers immediately asked "How many pages do we have to take to get that guarantee?" Perhaps this cynicism was unjustified.

Like *Good Housekeeping*, *McCall's* guarantee began to be quoted on television. It would be hard to find a neater gadget for an advertiser to get double benefits, also for the advertiser, *McCall's* had another kind of guarantee. It announced in 1959 that by October, 1960 it would issue six million copies. *McCall's* announced that under Mr. Mayes' editorship there would be vast changes. By the issue of November, 1959, these began to show. The November, 1959, issue stands for flash, brash, splash.

Since 1958 Mr. Samuel I. Newhouse, who owned a large chain of newspapers, bought control of the Condé Nast (*Vogue*, etc.) and Street and Smith (*Redbook, McCall's*). These magazines now have huge capital behind them. It is my opinion that while a lot of new money can be very helpful what the women's magazines need a lot of new ideas.

It looks exciting partly because of the screaming but clever head-lines and it has an air of confusion and hurry, due to a continual change of sizes and kinds of type and a variety of page arrange-ments. But its most striking feature is its use of color. This is truly superb. The magazine takes full advantage of its possibilities with bleed-off pages and stunning photography. To the hypnotic appeal of lavish lovelies the hasty reader lends herself as a willing sub-ject. She is rarely sufficiently critical to realize: "This is what I'd like to be, but what I shall never be."

Here we see the advertising mind leading the way and the maga-zine following. This superb use of color and design has been used by advertisers for years. Now the editors of *McCall's* have em-ployed them most skillfully as a basic means to glamorize realism. To me a magazine with such huge illustrations is difficult to read, especially when coupled with so many different sizes and forms of type. However the editors may not expect anybody to *read* the magazine. They know what the picture is worth.

The vast spreads of color should delight the advertisers. The idea here is not so much to sell the goods directly to the reader, rather to design material which can be used by the advertiser in a big, striking spread to send to the dealer. But certainly *McCall's* cannot overlook the fact that *Good Housekeeping, U.S. News* and *New Yorker* pages are smaller and that these periodicals appeal heavily to the advertiser. The *New Yorker* and *U.S. News* are the most successful phenomena in the advertising world. They are so heavily crowded with advertising that they have sometimes been called "dolls" within the trade.

Much of the reading matter in the "new" *McCall's* is sensible, but none of it is startling. It has something of the same everyday serviceability that had always distinguished *Good Housekeeping*. Under Mr. Mayes' editorship the word "Togetherness" has not been dropped, but it no longer means specifically man and wife.

It now vaguely includes everybody with a loud hello and a hearty slap on the back.

In these later issues *McCall's* is leaning toward big names. Eleanor Roosevelt's page has been retained. She answers questions, as always, and, looking these over, I wonder if the magazine chooses questions that, when answered, make her more than ever just "one of us women"? To offset this homely contribution, there is a new department by Clare Booth Luce which will report on the "political" woman. But one cannot help feeling that the bigger and better names are being asked or are going to be asked in littler and lesser ways, thus reducing the already small amount of useful and practical information which the magazine contains. This, however, remains to be seen.

There is an article showing how *McCall's* Use-Tests an automobile. No make of the car is mentioned, but I think many car owners could figure out which car was being tested. And some of the old tone of insincerity, of the we-girls-snickering-in-the-corner, can be detected in the following: "Of course, we also let husbands drive it to make sure it's an all-around family car."

Under its "Building Department," *McCall's* in 1959 showed a house in California with three bedrooms and quoted a price of $12,150. This is "cost of house without land in San Diego, California." The plans specify electrical wiring, plumbing (two whole baths), heat lamp in master bath, etcetera. All this for $12,150! There should be a stream of homemakers demanding this generous plan—but they'd better have a little extra money stashed away (Remember *Mr. Blandings Builds His Dream House?*)

All through Mr. Mayes' editorship of *Good Housekeeping*, the magazine was restrained in the use of sex, and there was less emphasis on woman's trickery than there was in the other magazines. But during the same period there was much more of both in *McCall's*. Perhaps, therefore, the following was left over from an earlier management. Under the caption: "Blue Jean Biology" in *McCall's* for September, 1959, this appeared:

> The bobby-soxer herself, Miss Junior Miss, is endowed by a mysterious but obviously prudent nature with more slowly excitable sex responses. She has more to fear from her heart than from her hormones. The danger in her case is that if doin' what comes naturally is what it takes to keep a blossoming Romeo on the hook, she's sometimes tempted to give in—against her better judgment true; but she should remember what good intentions pave the way to. . . . Quicker than a penguin sliding down an icicle—that's how quick a petting session can turn into a jam session. And you're the one in a jam.
>
> Troubles are like photographs. They are developed in dark places. Sitting for hours in a dark room or a parked car and kiss-kiss-kissing is ask-ask-asking for trouble. Prolonged kissing is more frustrating than having seasickness and lockjaw at the same time. It's the first step in serious love-making. It whets the appetite. It's meant to warm up the engines in preparation for a trip to the moon on gossamer wings. And once the engine is warmed up, it's rugged trying to turn it off.

You see, it is on the highest moral grounds, all this! But isn't it, in itself, likely to "whet the appetite?" Maybe I am just a cynic though, because the November issue of the magazine publishes these two presumably typical comments: One from the head of a hospital reads:

> I am a director of a sixty-one-bed hospital-residence for unmarried mothers. We are continuously filled to capacity, and have a waiting list. Most of our girls are from the typical American family, from every background and environment. Thank you for publishing this article.

The other is from a Superintendent of Public Schools:

> High Schools are plagued with pregnancies and forced high-school marriages. We feel that this article is the best thing we have seen dealing constructively with the problem, because it is written in language

the teen-agers accept. It should go farther than the advice of the family doctor or the health worker. Our homemaking teachers are making use of it and have had the girls secure copies.

The kindest thing I could say about these two letters is that "their writers" are naive about aphrodisiacs in words.

On the pattern illustrations, the magazine has departed from past usage. For one thing, they are photographed on live models, all dancing! Some detail is lost in the movement. But girls who make their own clothes tell me that this new way of showing patterns puts life into the clothes and that they get the details from the actual patterns.

In some respects the magazine carefully follows tradition, as, for example, the inclusion of a mushy sob-story about Babs Hutton. However, the most unexpected item in the November, 1959, issue is a practical and specific article on how to stop smoking by Arthur King. The first step, says the article, is to change your favorite brand of cigarette. Other advice in the article in many respects follows my own experience when I stopped smoking several years ago. (As one who used to smoke over two-and-a-half packs a day, I am interested in the present success of the filter. When I began to think I was smoking too much, I also began to use a filter, with the idea of cutting down. Of course I didn't! I stopped smoking by stopping abruptly.)

What makes this article of particular interest, however, is not simply the advice given, but that the subject is treated directly and without tongue-in-cheek. Dr. King is a consultant on alcohol problems and he treats the cigarette problem as though it were an alcohol problem. He divides smokers into categories: the light smoker, the medium smoker, the heavy smoker and the addicted smoker. But Dr. King is not a crusading Edward Bok, is at liberty to use the magazine to campaign against tobacco. That crusading era is past. Indeed, for one such practical and specific article, today there are thousands of cigarette advertisements and television commercials. Even human nature seems to favor the advertisers. For cigarette sales are far higher today than they were before lung cancer studies came along. Another example of how even the most unfavorable publicity is better than no publicity at all. A cynical friend of mine suggests that some enterprising tobacco company would make a fortune by advertising: "Our cigarettes give you more and better lung cancer!"

The third magazine which put strong emphasis on its "commendation seal" was *Parents' Magazine*. It is not quite a guarantee, but is worded:

> Commended by The Consumer Service Bureau of *Parents' Magazine*. Products eligible for *Parents' Magazine's* Commendation Seal are awarded the Seal only after *Parents' Magazine's* Technical staff and/or medical consultants have studied them and the claims made for them. The United States Testing Company, Inc. is employed on an annual retainer to do whatever tests are required.

> *Parents' Magazine* publishes the advertisements only of products and services which it believes to be suitable for families with children. Through its Consumer Service Bureau, products and services are conscientiously evaluated for their quality and usefulness.
> Readers are advised to consult their physicians concerning advertised pharmaceuticals for which health and therapeutic claims are made.

Nothing is said here about how many pages the advertiser must order in order to be "commended."

Editorially *Parents' Magazine* has had a powerful influence on women. On the whole, its contents have been carefully chosen. For instance, there was a contest on the subject "Why Children Go Wrong." The results were not sensational, but they were sensible, as in the following reasons given by the contestants:

Lack of discipline.
Lack of companionship between parents and children.
Parents too absorbed in their own interests.
Divorce, broken homes and disagreements between parents.
Lack of respect of the child's personality.
Poorly supervised reading, movies, dances and theatres.

The publisher of *Parents' Magazine,* George J. Hecht, who does not believe that bushels should be used to hide lights, calls himself the "man who raised ten million kids."

There was a good deal of turnover on the staff. Mr. Hecht said much of the magazine was devoted to pregnancy and childbirth and apparently this seemed to have the effect of producing "expectant" editors—they kept having to go because of coming babies.

Some of the authors in these early issues were hardly reliable. But the magazine, through the years, improved.

The *Parents' Magazine* Guarantee of Approval is not as specific as it once was; in many instances it places in confusion the distinction between a guarantee and a recommendation. "We recommend" and "we guarantee," once two quite different expressions, have become nearly synonymous. Even those magazines which still do *guarantee,* place many more conditions, restrictions and reservations upon the terms of their guarantee. Yet, the American public seems to rely upon these "guarantees of approval," and they have proven, in almost every instance, a boon to magazine circulation.

Specialization

Godey's Lady's Book had established a pattern. Then came the *Delineator* with a popularization of that pattern. In 1889 Edward Bok shot adrenalin into the women's magazines. For more than a generation the Bok idea flourished. Circulations sky-rocketed, advertising flowed.

Then the giants began to fumble. *Pictorial Review* and *Delineator* folded. The reason was simple. Women had changed. There had been profound changes in their habits, in the actual daily living of all Americans. The women's magazines had failed to adjust to these changes. The editors knew that the old pattern that had worked for nearly fifty years had lost its magic. But, trained in the Bok formula, they were afraid to leave it.

As usual when there is a change in business climate, the giants were the last to adjust to it. So, the *Ladies' Home Journal, Woman's Home Companion* and others kept on in the old way. There were changes in the staff, but the new editors, better educated than their predecessors, and carrying all the attitudes of intellectuals (and too often, social workers), looked in the wrong direction. They depended too much on the lure of big names, and paid fabulous prices for name people. But all this was fumbling. They worked and thought and had graphs made—the graphs were smoke-screens for their lack of intuition and imagination. With the Bok pattern now stale, there was no bell-wether for the flock to follow.

One of their major errors was in not giving sufficient attention to the younger woman. Editors were still accepting the mores of the past when mothers decided what their daughters should have. (There were articles about the young girl and the older girl here and there, but the assumption was that the mother had the final say.) They refused to accept the idea that the younger women were in revolt. This is ironical, because many of the editors were themselves young women in revolt. Unfortunately, however, they considered themselves above the ruck of democratic life. What was good for them, they thought, could hardly be what was best for other young women. Their own was a special situation. Besides, other young women weren't ready for independence yet.

But, ready or not, throughout the United States, girls in their teens and early twenties were in revolt. They were making up their own minds about fashions and clothes and morals. This swing away from the mother's control has gone so far that now teenagers seem to rule the woman's world.

Then in 1937 *Mademoiselle* shot into the skies. Its editors knew that young women wanted their say, that their problems were not the same as their mothers'. Also that young women didn't have so much money to spend, that they wanted several inexpensive dresses rather than one really good one. The success of *Mademoiselle* was sensational. *Mademoiselle* was the first to see that the blanket coverage of the women's field had seen its day, and that the time had come for specialization, for special appeals to a limited audience. *Mademoiselle, Charm, Parents' Magazine, Glamour* were all part of this and their success was notable. It seems odd, in the face of this, that the general women's magazines stuck to their old pattern.

Vogue and *Harper's Bazaar* had preceded *Mademoiselle*. They had limited themselves to high fashions but they did not limit themselves to a special audience as did *Mademoiselle*. They expected to reach the snob in all classes and for a while they did. Neither of these two was of much importance until about 1913. Then Hearst bought *Harper's Bazaar* (*Bazar* was the original spelling; it was later changed to *Bazaar*) and from that time it took an important place as a fashion mentor to the American woman. After Edna Woolman Chase became editor, *Vogue* took the lead away from *Harper's Bazaar* partly because of its excellent pattern business. Both magazines were known in the trade as the "rags," indicating the cynical attitude toward high-priced clothes within the trade. In their contents they were the acme of snobbishness, and at least at *Vogue,* that snobbishness extended to its internal management. It was a policy there to offer low salaries to new employees with the remark: "You know of the prestige that it means to work on *Vogue*." Both magazines were extravagantly handsome. Both were devoted to the French leadership in fashions. While clothes led their parade, they naturally had articles on cosmetics, on manners, and on protocol. Some space was given to other subjects, but always on the angle of "who's being talked about." But this was just the trimming. Their real purpose was to set the standards of fashion and usually of the highest-priced fashions.

With the spread of good ready-made clothes, the influence of "the rags" grew less. *Women's Wear,* which is a trade paper for manufacturers and department store buyers, also had fashion experts in Europe, and their information, as it had to be, was more practical and down to earth than that of *Vogue* and *Harper's Bazaar*. Most women without much money to spend were likely to glance hastily through *Vogue* and *Harper's Bazaar* in the beauty parlor. *Vogue's* patterns, which were somewhat less elegant than were the clothes featured in the magazine itself, were practical and successful.

About 1930 *Vogue* slipped badly and was taken over by Wall Street interests. Until that date the *Vogue* group had been owned by Condé Nast and his friends. When Wall Street took over, it kept the Nast name. Other publications owned then and later by the Condé Nast group were *House and Garden, Vogue Pattern Book, Glamour* and *Brides.* To this was added a large and highly profitable printing plant at Greenwich, Conn., which printed a number of other magazines, including the *New Yorker.*

In 1958 the whole business was bought by S. I. Newhouse, a newspaper publisher. In 1959 Mr. Newhouse became one of the biggest publishers in the world when he purchased Street and Smith, Inc., which owned *Charm,* among other publications.

Harper's Bazaar, for some time carried along by other more profitable Hearst magazines, had already begun to specialize in high grade fiction, some of the best in the country. But the specializing of *Vogue* and *Harper's Bazaar* had no influence to speak of on the other women's magazines, so that when *Mademoiselle* emerged in 1937, it signaled a wholly new departure.

About 1935 it had become apparent that the enormous number of young women working either out of or in the home, had totally different ideas from those of the older women. Because of that, *Mademoiselle* became at once a most striking success. It was published for women between the ages of eighteen and twenty-nine and was entirely practical. Its popular-priced fashions were its main subject. It constantly stuck to the low-priced goods that the readers could afford. For instance, on reducing diets, it headlined "Supermarket Diet" with a subhead, "Eat All You Can Carry Home, Lose Five Pounds." It gave more space than the older magazines to movies and jazz, and had lively though trivial fiction.

On sex it has been outspoken. In the issue of July, 1959, there was an article, "A Report On Current Attitudes Toward Chastity." One sentence in that article quoted an alumna of an eastern college as follows: "I don't think coming to a marriage pure has any positive virtue in itself. Sexual behavior is something you have to decide quite personally." Also quoted was another college girl, saying: "Except to the young and immature, and to those who are consecrated followers of their religious beliefs, chastity may no longer be an absolute virtue. But neither is sex. What is moral is not what is within the letter of the law—petting to orgasm versus intercourse, for example. What's moral to this generation is what contributes to the healthy growth of the individual involved." (More about how the other women's magazines treat sex in another chapter.)

Mademoiselle took the precaution of admitting editorially that these views did not represent the views of average Americans. But none the less, it allowed the views to be expressed in its pages.

Occasionally there was a table-talk piece on public affairs, and of course some information that was supposed to be helpful in showing the working girl how to get ahead. But these were merely slipped in between more important items. Make-up, clothes, a pretty face, a nice voice—they are *all-important*. Character, in the modern young women's magazines, is regarded with a cynical lift of the eyebrow.

In its own words, "*Mademoiselle* is addressed to young women between the ages of eighteen and thirty, an audience that is made up of college students, young women in their first jobs, and young-marrieds. A survey that *Time* magazine made has shown that three out of four of our readers are college-educated."

One of the innovations in *Mademoiselle* is this. Most of the women's magazines have a number of departments and cover each set of departments in each issue. *Mademoiselle* devotes most of its issues to one theme; one whole issue will be about the job, another to "young-marrieds" (what an awkward phrase!). Their top price for an article or a story is five hundred dollars, which is much lower than that of *Ladies' Home Journal*.

But here, as in other magazines for women, the main underlying idea was how to get your man and keep him, with, of course, more emphasis on the getting. The theme song sings loud. What normal girl between eighteen and thirty doesn't want a man? But it seems to me that many of the suggestions given about how to get a man would make it very difficult to keep him.

The amount of advertising in *Mademoiselle* was astounding. Some issues were so packed with advertising that much of it looked like editorial matter, and it was indeed difficult to tell them apart. When the women's magazines first began to have enormous circulations, they had been a most tempting market for advertisers. Never before had it been possible for an advertiser to reach *only women* for his products. But as these periodicals grew in number, they lost some of their allure for the advertiser. He could not possibly spend money enough to cover them all. Hence the *specialty* magazine, i.e., *Mademoiselle, Parents' Magazine, Brides* and even *My Baby*. Their success is not due alone to the interest of their readers, but to the fact that they could pinpoint the advertisers' money.

It is probable, since the advertisers must spend their money in more and more costly ways than ever before (especially with television), that the specializing magazines will have continued success, while the big general magazines will find the going harder. For the advertiser will probably no longer try to cover all avenues of approach to readers, but will choose those which will strike the highest percentage of the audience for his products.

So along came *Charm*. *Charm* kept its eye fixed on the armies of women with jobs, whether business or professional. As they put it, "*Charm's* readers represent a cross section of working women—married and single in all age groups." They say that they pay seventy-five to two hundred dollars for contributions. *Charm* has published much on how to get a job and hold it. This does not include anything to do with labor unions or wage scales. It does try in a tentative way to make the office worker more competent. This has severe limitations since anything real or thorough about becoming competent must not be included since it bores the readers. So, between the lines, *Charm* tells women how to get and hold their men against rough competition. Except for these minor differences, it is in content very much like *Mademoiselle*.

However, as a magazine specifically edited for women who work, *Charm* moved further with the tide. Of course, all the older editors knew that more and more married women worked; they did so themselves and their offices were staffed by working women. They knew too that their lives were different from that of the average woman; they had to juggle at least four elements—home, office, marriage, and the special problem of being a woman. Editors who became pregnant kept on with their jobs, clad in bright, defiant raiment. Yet, even so, these same editors were not ready to come out and say flatly, "We working women live different lives." The effort was all in the other direction, to prove that the working woman could be like the home-staying woman.

But if *Charm* failed to represent truly what it professed to represent, in the inner circle of its staff it became almost a way of life. Its offices had charm, its staff looked charming, and its people dressed with charm.

The third magazine of this type was *Glamour*. It carried more fashions than any of the others, which was natural since it was a sort of stepchild of *Vogue*. Everything else in it was a side issue. On the line of "get your man," it had articles on "Fashions Seen by Men" in which an editor of the *Harvard Crimson* and another of the *Princeton Tiger* told what the boys liked about the girls. One of these began, "Girl-watching is not an exact science." This young man classified girls. Some of his classifications were: "The Black-Stocking," "Booktoter," and "The Tight-Skirted Eye-catcher." It is a pleasure to include in this book some male silliness too.

When Condé Nast Publications bought the Street and Smith publications, they announced that *Glamour* and *Charm* would be combined into one magazine, and the combined circulation would be 1,315,000 copies. This seemed to be good practical business sense, since the magazines are much alike and they appeal, more or less, to the same age group.

But the younger girls needed something, too. Hence *Seventeen.* The young girls were in rebellion. They preferred tight slacks and shorts even though they were hot and uncomfortable, because their mothers had worn skirts. *Seventeen* was understandably more cautious in content than the other specialty magazines, since most of its readers are a good bit younger than seventeen. Yet it needed something as a standard. So, its be-all and end-all was the "date." One piece reads: "What! No Date?" Its theme was if you don't have a date, then do something such as read, write letters, start a diary. But a date comes first.

Another theme was that parents were to be shown their place, as in a piece entitled "Divorce's Child—Why Don't Parents Grow Up." And on the "date" theme, a two-page spread "He's Not So Bad Even If . . . he is over-quiet or has to work while in school," and "She's Not So Bad Even If . . . she does wear glasses or has early curfew or she gets better marks than you do." And "The American Diamond," the theme being "if you're a girl and don't know about baseball, you can go hide during the baseball season or have fun by learning to enjoy the game."

Seventeen says there are nine million teen-age girls whom they call "gold-getters." The teenager is also a gold giver—not only the money she spends herself, but what her parents spend for her. Probably the most spoiled individual in America is the sixteen-year-old girl in a family with a little money to spend.

A special magazine for brides was part of the Condé Nast stable. The average age of the bride in this country is from eighteen to twenty, and most girls think this is the only day when they can shine. To quote the television program, she'll be "Queen For A Day." So naturally the chief contents of the magazine *Brides* are clothes, protocol, and romance, pretty much in that order.

All these magazines have had something they called "sophistication." This was played up in the fiction, which on the whole was not bad. Many were second-string short stories by well-known and highly regarded writers.

Next to fashions, the most important subject in all these magazines has been reducing. Each new diet as it comes along is treated as a miraculous new discovery. Then in a little while there is a totally different diet, again a miracle. Fortunately, some of the diets are harmless. Some are perhaps helpful. Some are bad and even dangerous, according to the American Medical Association. The Association's Counsel on Foods and Nutrition has warned against the indiscriminate use of new low-protein diets. The main emphasis in the later 1950's had shifted into the field of exercise.

One of the tendencies in the 1950's seemed to me most unhealthy, and that was weight reducing for teenagers.[1] They are still growing girls and they can be dangerously injured by denial of

[1] From the *New York Times* of October 11, 1959:

"Youngsters are often subjected to the taunts and ridicule of schoolmates, as well as to intense parental pressures. They are bribed: 'Lose ten pounds and you'll get a new wardrobe.' They are threatened: 'You'll never get married unless you lose weight!' They are nagged, spied upon and regarded as generally irresponsible. From all sides, their sense of self-esteem is subjected to assault."

food. Many teenagers have a little adolescent plumpness, which disappears later by itself. Naturally no woman is more susceptible to the dream of being a skinny model than the teen-age girl. She is so anxious to please the boys that she is willing to go on a risky reducing diet and even to take risky and dangerous medicines. Little can be done about these delusions of teenagers, but it seems too bad that magazines should encourage it. They encourage it too, of course, in older women, but they are supposed to have some responsibility—to know better (even if they don't).

Fashions in all these specialty magazines are of first importance. In *Mademoiselle, Glamour* and *Charm* they are sensible and practical. To many men the continual changing of women's fashions seems wasteful and foolish. H. L. Mencken had a "minority report" on this:

Women yield to the current fashions, however preposterous, because they are too realistic to try to conceal their natural human inclination to dress up, to strike the public eye with arresting gauds, to give a show of wealth and consequence, always impressive to people in general. Women know how such a display is admired and envied, and how much envy may be worth . . . in deference and respect.

In this respect I am altogether with my fellow women. In the days when a new dress cost a fortune and when diamonds were a sign of wealth, few women could afford to dress fashionably. I wonder if the changing fashions do not serve the same purpose . . . and much more cheaply. Most American women can buy at least one new dress in a current fashion, which proves to the onlooker that she is in the chips, a much cheaper way to do so than with a diamond necklace. Fashion and vanity became a little less costly and beneficial to a larger group of women.

There is a delusion that *all* women like beautiful clothes, even love them. Only the vainest of women *love* beautiful clothes. I have observed that nearly always a successful designer or authority on woman's clothes is a good-looking woman and was a beautiful girl. Her first interest in clothes came from the mirror, from seeing herself dressed up. With most women, clothes, though of major importance, are used for a purpose, "to look right, to make an impression, to establish her place in the world."

One aspect is so noticeable that it seems beyond argument. Women of superior taste in art frequently seem to have no feeling about clothes. They often prefer clothes that are "out of style." The fact is that fashion and taste have nothing to do with each other. Beauty in clothes could be the same throughout the centuries but the talent which picks out what is going to be fashionable is something especial. In a way it might be compared to choosing from a number of songs which is likely to be "the hit tune."

Probably the biggest racket in all the women's magazine field is the beauty stuff. I'm told that millions of women buy these magazines for their beauty advice. There seems always to be something new on the subject, but very little worth the paper it's printed on. It is, I am sure, too much to expect the women's magazines to throw out the enormous revenue they get from cosmetics. Yet that is what they would have to do if they told the story of cosmetics truly.

Take the business of face masks. Grandmother (of the present generation) spread the white of an egg over her face and got as good results as any mud pack could have given her. Today's cosmetics are simply more pleasant to use. Where great-grandma used mutton fat, today's girl has a pleasant-smelling cold cream.

There is endless chi-chi about expensive cream. Many a woman is cleaning her face with cream when her skin would be better off with soap and water. Few creams have the cleansing quality of an old-fashioned steam treatment with boiling water, which, except for an occasionally extra-dry skin, is unquestionably the finest cleanser in the world.

There seems to be social status in the use of expensive cosmetics. When a woman's friends see a long string of this high-priced waste on her dressing table, she feels she's "in."

All these magazines considered only the woman under the age of thirty. There was a theory, well-founded, that the biggest markets for advertisers were in the ages between thirteen and thirty, with heavy emphasis on the teenagers. The woman between forty and fifty-five has been ignored. Yet she can be valuable both as a reader and as a target for advertisers. Her family has grown up and gone off. She has more time on her hands than she knows what to do with. She may use it to re-decorate her home, to buy new furniture to replace that which has become shabby from years of use. She has more money to spend than she had when raising her family. She likes to look nice but the fashion parade ignores her. As one woman said to me, "I couldn't even find an idea for a dress to wear when my daughter got married."

These specialty magazines, *Mademoiselle* and *Charm-Glamour,* had no foolish notions about trying to win the man of the family. In an advertisement in 1959, *Charm-Glamour* promised, "All things irrelevant to men, important to women." This idea is almost basic to continued success for a woman's magazine. The slogan "Togetherness" used so persistently by *McCall's Magazine* has value as an attention getter, but it can hardly attract men readers, which was its original objective.

There are two more magazines which belong under the classification of women's publications though they pretend to be for general household use. They are *House and Garden* and *House Beautiful*. They are slick and handsome. Their thesis is spend, spend, spend. And in reality they are simply elegant advertising brochures and I think that takes care of that.

12

Getting Down to Brass Tacks

In the midst of all this proliferation of big magazines, big pictures, magnificent photography, big names, there appeared a publication so small and modest that the others, if they saw it at all, looked down their noses. It was a slim little something given away at A & P stores. It was called *Woman's Day* and was destined to become a powerful force in increasing democracy among American women. And, like the supermarkets themselves, it helped to change the habits of the American family.

Another publication, *Family Circle*, was already being distributed in other chains, as was *Everywoman* (now combined with *Family Circle*). But it did not then have the boldness or quality of *Woman's Day* and it created no stir. These magazines were sold only in a selected list of stores. They had few or no subscriptions and no newsstand sale. *Woman's Day* soon became the best and most important. For practical sense, straightforward attitude, it was, to my mind, the best of all women's magazines. In 1959, however, *Family Circle* had grown up and in some issues was better than *Woman's Day*. It has indeed become difficult to tell the two magazines apart. *Family Circle* imitates *Woman's Day* and *Woman's*

Day imitates *Family Circle* . . . a procedure that is not peculiar among women's magazines.

One curious difference between the two magazines is that *Woman's Day* is edited by a staff of women, while *Family Circle's* editors are men. This may account for the fact that *Family Circle* leans more toward humor and excellent fiction. *Woman's Day* seems to have less humorous material and good fiction than was the rule under Mabel Souvaine (a contradiction of what I just said about male editors, since she is a woman after all.) The truth is that it is impossible to weigh editorial differences between the men and the women in this field. The two greatest editors were Sarah Josepha Hale and Edward Bok. Today's *Ladies' Home Journal* is edited by a man and wife, *McCall's* by a man, *Vogue* by a man, *Harper's Bazaar* by a woman, *Good Housekeeping* by a man, *Mademoiselle* by a woman.

According to James Playsted Wood, in his *Magazines in the United States,* "The store distributed magazines do not have the prestige of the big name women's periodicals, nor the awesomeness of great reputation. Possibly for this reason, they seem more approachable to many of their readers . . . a simpler reason, women like what they see pictured and described in the magazine's pages and want it."

Woman's Day, as it now exists, was conceived by two executives of the A & P stores. This was during the depression in the thirties when women were looking at both sides of every nickel. It seemed to the two men, Frank Wheeler and Donald P. Hanson, that if the menu sheet the stores were giving away was expanded into a magazine, it could be useful; but the magazine must cost so little that the customer would not feel it; hence *Woman's Day* was for sale at A & P counters for two cents a copy.

Later, with increased demand and size the price was raised to five cents, then to seven cents. At this writing, it is on sale for ten cents, which, when you figure it out, isn't so much more than two cents in actual buying power. (*Family Circle* has also become a ten-cent magazine.)

The store-distributed magazines had none of the back-and-bank breaking problems of getting circulation that pester the higher priced media in their field. *Woman's Day* continued small until 1943, when Mabel Hill Souvaine became its editor and remained so for fifteen years. Under her management the magazine grew in circulation to nearly five million. During this period there were many temptations to go far afield from its original purpose. But both the publishers and the editors insisted that the first function of a magazine for women was to be useful. For instance, in no way did *Woman's Day* imitate the *Ladies' Home Journal*. *Woman's Day* was edited for the millions of women who had to watch pennies, who did their own housework. Such a woman wants to look nice, but she cannot go all out for any new fashions. What she wears has to be something that will stay in style for quite a while. She thinks, "I can't have everything. I'll do as well as I can."

The editors were careful never to write down to their readers (a practice common in the big women's publications). They never thought of their circulation as "the masses" and when they gave them fiction, they kept to an intelligent standard. In spite of the connection with the A & P stores, the magazine operated under strict rules. These stores had nothing to say about its contents or its policy. There was no editorial publicity for any advertiser. Above all, there was nothing that could be considered a plug for a chain store. The supermarket was never mentioned, the very word was taboo, even in fiction.

Woman's Day was edited from within. Most magazines' content is picked up from material sent in on speculation by writers and agents. The articles are published without investigation and often with naive confidence in an author's reputation. *Woman's*

Day also had the largest, most elaborate testing laboratories of any woman's magazine, although *Good Housekeeping* disputes this. And, as part of its policy, the magazine emphasized "How to Do It." In 1947 this became a separate section, "How to Make It—How to Do It—How to Fix It." Every item was tried out in the magazine's workrooms, then the reader was told How to Get the dress, or the dresser or the curtains or the garden . . . whatever it might be. No effort was made to outreach the practical to attain an ideal. For instance, when Cornell University began its campaign for seat belts in automobiles, the temptation in most magazines was to run this as a news story or a propaganda piece. But *Woman's Day* sent its chief technician, William Whitlock, to Cornell University to find out how the belts could be made at home at a cut in cost.

Anything coming under the heading of service was never bought; it was built, tested and tried within *Woman's Day* organization. Even when they suggested a plan for a house, they built the house.

A popular feature was the Collector's Cookbook. This was a series of recipes printed on narrower pages than the rest of the magazine and on heavier paper. It was bound so that it could easily be taken out and preserved. Some of the recipes in this section were excellent. They were all supposed to be tested in the magazine's own laboratories. In September, 1959, this separate section was devoted to sauces for spaghetti. Here the recipes sometimes slipped from their former standards of excellence. A recipe entitled "Meat Sauce" and another "White Anchovy Sauce" are good. However there is the temptation to bigness. The editors, trying to put in too many recipes, used some that are doubtful. A sauce of bacon and corn seems absurd as a trimming for spaghetti. Two others which seemed poor are the "Deviled Ham Sauce" and the "Watercress Sauce."

In October, 1959, this separate detachable section was devoted to eggs. Recipes for Cuban and Puerto Rican eggs (good ones) showed how closely *Woman's Day* kept in touch with its "plain people" readers. The omelette recipe included milk, which to this writer is a sin against cookery, but that is a matter of taste. On the whole, however, the kitchen aspect of *Woman's Day* has stood up well.

For years it was the policy of *Woman's Day,* when clothes were shown, to have them made up to order first. This policy has been changed. Since the fashions in 1959 were planned to sell patterns for its home-dressmaking audience, these patterns had to be fairly pedestrian. Yet only a skillful tailor could make the suits that were shown in September, 1959.

There was an appealing department called "More Clothes for Less Money," but some of its instructions were puzzling. For instance: "If you have to add three inches to the bust line, you sketch a three-quarter increase along each seam edge starting at bottom of armhole and continuing down to and including the waistline." I am told that you cannot increase any seam by more than one-half an inch without losing the original line of the dress.

Naturally, as part of the common-sense advice there were pieces about diet, but no queer reducing schemes. There was material about child care, beauty, various subjects in which the family would be interested, but nowhere was there an effort made to push women into activities for which they were unprepared. The editors thought that the pontifical attitude so characteristic of women's magazines should be avoided. As a consequence, its readers felt more friendly toward it than toward its big competitors.

There were very few medical articles. Medical articles are one of the worst plagues of the women's magazines. As anyone knows who has talked to a good doctor, the medical world is genuinely upset by the clashing, dashing and irresponsible publication of untested medical "news."

Woman's Day thought that it should not try to handle people's lives and so avoided articles dealing with emotional problems. Watered-down, contorted Freud is another pest or pestilence in most women's magazines. Such articles are usually rash in their freely-given free advice, and in every case are without personal knowledge of the individual. Often the writer is not properly trained in the field.

The editors also avoided articles on sex. They decided that if they were going to avoid the watered-down Freud, it was only consistent to eliminate sex articles and thereby avoid watered-down Kinsey. I should like to point out here that much of the criticism of other magazines in this chapter did not apply to *Good Housekeeping,* which had all along had many of the same sensible attitudes as *Woman's Day.*

In the last few years *Woman's Day* has abandoned some of these basic principles, though a great deal in the magazine remains sound. There is a tendency toward making the same glib know-it-all pronouncements that have made the big women's magazines so false. There is also a tendency to withdraw somewhat from the service and testing idea of its original policy. This seems to me unfortunate.

Both *Woman's Day* and *Family Circle* are published in separate geographical sections with varying prices and advertising rates for different parts of the country. This appeals strongly to advertisers who push different products in different places, or whose products are regional either in use or popularity. *Family Circle* has had far more of these sections, but it is probable that *Woman's Day* now under Fawcett ownership and distribution outside the A & P stores will also have more of these divisions. What effect the new ownership will have on the contents of the magazine remains to be seen.

Over all, these new magazines distributed through grocery stores have been huge successes both in their influence on their readers and as money-makers. It is therefore a comfort to know that they are, with the exception of *Good Housekeeping,* less showy, less pretentious and more sensible than the big women's magazines.

13

S-E-X

In the 1940's, the women's magazines began to fight for their lives; their life blood, advertising, was flowing into radio and television. But there remained one area where they had an advantage; they could and did print stuff about sex which would be censored off the air waves. The women's magazines had always sold sex, but they had done it in a prim, prissy style. Now they were changing sex to S-E-X. The new come-on had to wear false faces. One of these was "Health and Sex," one was "Platform-Lecture Sex," another was "Sex for the Good of the Community" and still another, "Worrying about the Teenager Sex." [1]

Woman's Day and *Family Circle* resisted the temptation, and *Good Housekeeping* approached it with reserve, running articles only occasionally and with some taste. However, *Woman's Home Companion, McCall's* and *Ladies' Home Journal* abandoned taste and after a while abandoned the false faces.

[1] In 1959, one T.V. program at 1 A.M., began to edge in, but not very far.

James Playsted Wood in his book *Magazines in the United States,* writes in a manner sometimes etched with acid. He says:

The basic subject of most of the editorials (in the women's magazines) is sex in domesticated guise—how to get, train, and keep a husband; why this marriage failed and this one succeeded; how to bring up your children; what to ask the doctor; and all the rest. The basic approach is that of flattery. The great success of women's magazines in this country seems to have been due in large part to the acumen of publishers and editors in realizing that they can more profitably address women as women rather than women as people. Men like Bok were shrewd enough to realize that the mass of women applaud rather than resent the distinction, and his successors have wisely followed the same policy.

In November, 1945, the *Ladies' Home Journal* came out with a blast against syphilis. Perhaps the editors assumed their readers couldn't find a doctor to consult. Perhaps their readers' P.T.A. or other clubs had never heard of syphilis. Perhaps they thought their children ought to know about this danger and that it would be a good idea for them to pick up the knowledge from the magazine on the library table. After all, what a handy way to let the youngsters (in 1947) read "Abortion is an Ugly Word." Or, perhaps, if they wanted to let the youngsters know why mother had such a short temper, they could have read in the *Ladies' Home Journal* "What Makes Wives Dissatisfied" or "Our Sexual Dilemma." By 1951, the children, now four years older, could learn about "The Art of Married Love."

I wonder why the reader couldn't ask her doctor instead? Perhaps she preferred taking such judgment on the authority of someone she didn't know. And perhaps her doctor (in November, 1947) would have been astonished to read, "We Could Banish Venereal Disease in Nine Days." It seems to me, however, little surprising that in October, 1959, The American Medical Association announced that gonorrhea was increasing. It seems the natural result.

But perhaps I do the editors an injustice. Perhaps they were really worried about venereal disease and the art of married love. At any rate, only six months later, they ran an article, "The Smut Peddler is After Your Child." (They were of course not referring to the smut they themselves were peddling.) And, with a straight face, in 1952, they were able to run a piece entitled, "Are Women in Uniform Immoral?"

Medical information has been an excuse for any amount of smut. The *Ladies' Home Journal* published "Chastity and Syphilis," "Promiscuity and Venereal Disease," "Combat Fatigue in Marriage." (Not meant to be funny).

Then there was a piece on lady-like sex, with the subtitle "Is Morality Normal?"

In 1947 Dr. Alfred C. Kinsey had burst upon the American public with *Sexual Behavior in the Human Male.* This was later followed by similar studies on the human female. It is somewhat startling to realize how many learned books Kinsey wrote without causing a ripple on such subjects as "The Gall Wasp," "Genus Cynips," "Introduction to Biology," "Edible Wild Plants in Eastern North America."

First, the Kinsey reports had to be sufficiently dramatized; after that, a kind of watered-down Kinsey took over. In 1954 the *Ladies' Home Journal* seemed to fall into a kind of printed soap opera pattern, with articles in a new department on love and marriage. These pieces seemed singularly lacking in wisdom. Many of the themes were cheap enough for the most garish newsstand sales with themes like "I Love My Husband's Best Friend" and "I'm Tempted to Have An Affair." I suppose the following could have been put under the heading of news: "Teenagers and Sex in Australia."

But, cheer up! In September, 1958, *Ladies' Home Journal* took a stiff stand: In an article entitled, "Why Premarital Sex is Always Wrong," it practically insisted that premarital sex is *wrong*.

Ladies' Home Journal was by no means the lone offender in this rampage on sex. *Woman's Home Companion* went even farther out on the limb and was more extreme. But the *Woman's Home Companion* at least had some excuse. It knew it was in bad shape and apparently used S-E-X in a last desperate effort to get circulation. The results of such efforts, at best, were spasmodic. Perhaps the *Ladies' Home Journal* learned a lesson from the *Companion* because the *Journal's* tone became milder.

McCall's magazine had always used the *Journal* as a model, but they both came to sex at about the same time. In May, 1945, Philip Wylie was already saying in *McCall's* "Infidelity has become a serious moral problem among men in the service and women at home with dangerous implications for the future of American family life."

In 1947 we get a whisper at last of the coming great campaign of "Togetherness" in *McCall's*. In June of that year there was an article on "How He Goes Through The Menopause," with a subhead, "There is hope now in new drugs and new treatment for the man nobody understands." (Was Daddy coming into his own at last?)

Daddy was further welcomed into the family in the January, 1951, issue with "How Female is Your Husband." On the other hand, it might push Daddy right out of the family if the wife began to look with questioning eyes at the creature she had always loved because he was "all man." Care had to be taken in constructing a new man. This *man* had a woman's sensitivity hidden under a gruff, masculine exterior. In March, 1950, *McCall's* pulled heavily on medical privilege with, "Does a Pregnant Woman Who Has Syphilis Always Have a Syphilitic Baby?" This was a department headed, "The Questions You Ask the Doctor About Your Child." Like the *Ladies' Home Journal*, *McCall's* opened its pages wide to watered-down Kinsey. They ran a piece in 1955 called "Artificial Insemination . . . Legitimate or Illegitimate?" In April, 1957, there was "Women Without Men." For women in Berlin where the war left a heavy shortage of men, the article explained that "the fundamental problems are strictly animal: to find a mate, shelter and enough food to stay alive."

No comment of mine, no attempted irony could equal a bare list of the pieces run in *McCall's:*

January, 1958—"The Hundred and Twenty-Nine Ways to Get a Husband."

November, 1957—"If Your Man Goes Away"—You may be sexually frustrated but there are better remedies than promiscuous affairs and too much drinking. . . .

January, 1952—"Without a Bed"—Should a wife be blamed for selling her husband's bed because he told the neighbors she was a cold proposition?

February, 1958—"Why Men Desert Their Wives"—The main reason given was: "sexual maladjustment and infidelity (chiefly on the part of the husband)."

October, 1958—"Eighty-Four Ways to Make Your Marriage More Exciting"—In this, one suggestion for the husband was: "buy her sexy perfumes, let her buy *herself* the light floral scents." One suggestion for the wife was: "Buy a new negligee and wear it."

In 1959 Herbert R. Mayes became editor of *McCall's*. Since 1925 he had been editor of *Good Housekeeping*, where he ran a really superior woman's magazine with emphasis on the service departments. *Good Housekeeping* did little preaching, little telling women what they ought to do and published little on sex.

When a magazine gets a new editor, he cannot in one month make drastic changes. There is always material left over from the previous management, material that has been paid for, or is already in type, or is contracted for. Perhaps that was why, in September, 1959, *McCall's* ran a tasteless headline, "What Is More Enticing Than a Woman's Legs?" This was a come-on for an article that turned out to be about hosiery. Also, under the classification of "Things My Mother Never Told Me or Blue-jean Biology," there was this: "Where the male critter is concerned, never are the hormones more frantic, more sensitive to excitement than during the teen years."

There can be no objection on the whole to the advice given in this article but does it have to be so crude, indeed brutal and cynical, in manner and language?

Raw as much of this stuff is, it is child's play to what has appeared in *Mademoiselle, Glamour* and *Charm.* In 1943, *Glamour* ran a piece by Bertrand Russell entitled "If You Fall In Love With a Married Man." He claimed: (1) "If you love the married man but he does not return your affections, go away." (2) "If you each love the other and he has no children and doesn't get along with his wife, and if you are both rational people, the man will get a divorce and marry you as soon as possible." (3) "At best, any girl who falls in love with a married man must expect misrepresentation and hostility from a small crowd of people whose chief joy in life seems to be to take sides in such situations."

Is *Glamour* here true to the women's magazine pattern of telling readers what to do even though it has to do it through the garrulous pen of Bertrand Russell? Command and exhortation are here again, but where before the command was toward restraint and perhaps on the prim side, now it is "no holds barred." Since *Glamour,* like *Mademoiselle* and *Charm,* appeals to women, so they say, between eighteen and thirty, one wonders at this readiness to advise and direct. How can they dare to take the responsibility for the lives of readers that this sort of material indicates?

However, it is true that this material is at least outspoken and doesn't have the weasel-like indirection of much sex material in other magazines. The *Ladies' Home Journal,* too, is more outspoken, especially in the department run by the late Dr. Abraham Stone. In one of his articles, there is this question: "What are the chief differences between a woman's and a man's sexual reactions?" The answer states in part: "The man, for instance, is more readily aroused sexually by psychologic stimuli, and he needs little direct stimulation and little preliminary love-play. For the woman, the major sources of arousal and satisfaction are the tenderness, the touch, the caress, the kiss, the embrace that is a part of love-making. . . . Usually a man cannot function sexually until he is fully aroused, while a woman may receive a man at any time, even if she has little or no desire."

All this makes perfectly good sense. But the women's magazines are usually left lying around the house so that I can well understand the reaction of those women who tell me that they have canceled subscriptions to various women's magazines because, "I don't like the kids reading all that sex."

One also wonders how these magazines dare to hand out orders and categorical advice on complex psychological problems, such as this problem of a reader in the *Ladies' Home Journal:* "My husband wanted me and the other woman too. He needed us both." This is being given out as absolute and unquestioned truth.

Of all the magazines *Mademoiselle* is the most outspoken and the most extreme. In the issue of July, 1959, there was an article entitled: "A Report on Current Attitudes Toward Chastity." Whether by accident or design the first page of this article is decorated by a key with a large circular head and an arrow which had the appearance of phallic symbol. An editor's note claimed that the article was based on interviews with graduates of or students at accredited colleges. Also that the people interviewed were not questioned about their own personal behavior. Further, the editors said that almost all the girls in college "were opposed to premarital sexual intercourse for themselves, while the majority of the college men favored premarital experience (for themselves)." With few exceptions both men and women graduates believed in "premarital relationships under appropriate circumstances."

The magazine then went on to give the opinions of some of the people interviewed:

"Self-assured young wives who have practiced their belief that sexual intercourse is a normal expression of love since they were in college claimed the above belief."

"Undergraduate men, while sheepishly admitting that they want their wives to be virgins, expressed the same view."

There are two ways to describe this material. One could call it "hall-bedroom sex" or one could call it "emotional development," as described in the following vague paragraph in the *Mademoiselle* article. "Sexual intercourse for me is a way of expressing love. I would give myself only to someone to whom I already belonged, someone I had known and loved for some time, someone with whom I shared attitudes and goals in life. . . . We would touch each other in many ways, not concealing or being ashamed of the way we are. We'd accept each other—strong and weak qualities— as we are. When two people can be that intimate the sexual part completes the closeness, and anything else would be pretense."

One girl said, "Sexual commitment is also an expression of faith in oneself." Another said, "I might be able to participate in a one-night affair but would feel *unsafe* in an extended relationship." Very odd.

The men interviewed about these various opinions and statements were not enthusiastic. They were doubtful about wanting or having girls with such attitudes for their wives But, on the other hand, they did not want to place restrictions on themselves.

As one boy expressed it, "I want to learn about sex for my own good. I will have to take advantage of every opportunity with girls who are the type you go out with for sex."

We repeat that *Mademoiselle* says it is directed toward women from eighteen to thirty, but neither on the cover (where this article is advertised) nor in any other place in the magazine do we find anything like, "Keep this issue away from girls from thirteen to eighteen." And, if it were there, it couldn't stop youngsters. I am not advancing any prudish or old-fashioned arguments about trying to keep the facts of life hidden from young women. For it is true that girls should know about what they are facing. But for goodness sake, not in a brazen, publicly advertised, half-baked fashion! Not in the screaming headlines of S-E-X, *S-E-X,* S-E-X!

14

The Apron Strings

"The American woman may be a tigress in Macy's basement, but she's a timid kitten in the voting booth." So said *Woman's Day* in October, 1958, in an article asking "Are American Women Backward Politically?" It went on to say: "They control the national economy; they hold majority (*sic*) of the power at the polls; they've proven themselves in business and the professions. Yet compared with other countries, they have an unimpressive political record."

True! The American woman has many sources of power. She spends more than half the money that goes for goods and services. She takes a large part in buying her husband's clothes. Her social influence is beyond measuring. She belongs to and has time to work for political organizations while men are on their jobs. For all the same reasons, she is more powerful than men in P.T.A. Why then is she a "timid kitten in the voting booth?" Even so, why does many a successful candidate boast: "I got in with the woman's vote"?

How to reconcile these two statements?

Quite simply. Women as a whole do not even try to understand the basic ideas of any party, much less of an individual candidate. A woman will listen bright-eyed to a political explanation only to forget it all the next day. This is not because she is stupid. Far from it. Usually she just doesn't have the basic knowledge or frame of reference to orient what she's learned. Scraps of knowledge do not build up to wisdom unless they can be related to a basic pattern. Many intelligent people, for instance, find that information about the atom or about space-science slips through their minds without taking hold because they have no basic scientific training to tie it to.

Understanding of political movements floats around aimlessly among the emotions unless it can be related to a background of solid historical knowledge. A knowledge of history is the foundation upon which political understanding is built. And, as a rule, women do not like history. They often write historical novels in which they throw a whole era into a silly love story. But it is startling to realize how few women write straight history.

The women's magazines, knowing their readers, seldom, if ever, run historical articles. Perhaps, once in a great while, some biography slips in. But the editors wisely pass by anything explaining historical movements or ideas. Say one candidate believes in centralized power at the top of government and the other believes in distributed local or individual power These ideas are merely words to a woman who cannot tie them in her mind even to such a clear-cut struggle as the Jefferson-Hamilton conflict.

Edward Bok, once in a while, tried a little history on his readers. The reaction was one of boredom, and indifference. Most women cannot recognize the value of history in one's present understanding and enjoyment of life. Only by measuring them against the great swings of history do the events of each day fall into their proper proportion. If you see that some event is at the bottom of the swing of history and you know enough to realize that the swing may start upward soon, you're not likely to be carried away by a trivial movement which appeals only to your heart.

Women political leaders would dispute me on this statement. One of them says that women know about issues and political affairs. She makes this claim because many belong to Republican or Democratic clubs and "if they read the mail and attend club meetings, they really know a great deal." In *U. S. News & World Report* of December 12, 1958, Mrs. Clare B. Williams, a political leader, stated that three million Republican women were working on the last presidential campaign. To the question: "What kind of work did they do?" she answered: "Well, they do all kinds of things. For one thing, women do the details of a campaign. It is women who sit in headquarters all over the country and address envelopes and stuff them. It is women who answer the telephone. It is women who hand out the campaign literature. It is women who ring doorbells. It is women who do the actual work in the precincts—door to door. It is the women who do the telephoning."

Did any of these three million take time out to think?

In the same magazine Mrs. Katie Louchheim, a Democratic leader, paints this picture: "George comes home and says, 'Now, look, you had time to go to these rallies and you've been to your meetings and you've seen some of these candidates. Now, whom shall we vote for?'"

To me, this seems more the exception than the rule. Much more likely he would say: "Have a nice time, dear? That's good. What have you got for dinner?" Or if he did ask, "Now, whom do we vote for?" the reply probably would convince him never to ask that question again.

But there is one subject on which a woman trusts her own judgment. She firmly believes that she can judge people by their looks. So she casts her vote for a man who "looks" honest or "looks" kind or, "Isn't he the best-looking thing you ever saw?" A deep masculine voice becomes a yardstick to test a man's ability.

One aspect of this that seems puzzling is that there aren't more women elected to office. Women seldom use their power to vote other women into office. I think perhaps that instinctively a woman distrusts another woman because she expects her to think like herself. It was a wry sort of joke in the campaign of 1956 which said: "Half the women were in love with Eisensower and half were in love with Stevenson."

One other angle of women's thinking is that they tend to be drawn toward any kind of rosy promise without searching for its effects. It is as though you were standing at the entrance of a long dark hall, and right in front of you there was a bright rosy light. If you pushed that light aside you would see where the long passage led to. But if you were dazzled by the rosy light (in other words, the immediate promise) the after-effects escaped you. And that might be very bad indeed.

It is this attitude that makes women so attractive. Their hearts are aglow with the immediate promise. They refuse to take into account the cost or the eventual results, insisting that the future will take care of itself. This "Ain't Gonna Rain No More" attitude is naturally nice to hear and pleasant to believe, which makes it especially tempting bait for women. Also, women have looked upon themselves as the doers of good deeds from the time in the past when the lady of the manor went about carrying baskets of food to poor people. This picture has been deeply imprinted in women's minds. That's all fine. But it leads to a kind of political thinking in which women are tempted by policies that put them in a similar position. Unfortunately, they do not use the caution which they would apply to their own money, since it is somebody else's money (their government's) that they are giving away.

Of course it isn't only in voting and politics that women throw away their power for an illusion. Most people know what happened to our schools in the last decade; how science, mathematics and logic were dropped and replaced by frills. To be sure, men had some share of the responsibility for this. Certainly they were responsible for over-emphasis on sports, but it is the women who have taken over the Parent Teacher's Association and other such organizations. And it is women who believe that nice manners, dancing, setting a pretty table—that such things are important. Therefore the larger share of the blame must go to the women and to their magazines, which always put false emphasis on frills.

The control of money (big money) has moved from the hands of men into the hands of women. Through inheritance and new opportunities, women are more and more powerful in the financial world. It is claimed that they now possess more wealth than men, and with their longer life expectancy, this control will probably become even more pronounced. Of course, a good deal of their money is still invested and spent with the advice of men. But it has become important to know how women handle these fortunes, what their attitudes are, if and how they differ from men in their relations to property, and in what kinds of investment they are most likely to place their trust. This has become of national importance.

In the continual growth of women's power, men were slowly pushed into the background. Daddy came to be endured or treated with amused condescension. Now women, scared by what they have accomplished, are making efforts to bring father back into the picture. Of course he may never have his previous stature, and women don't really repent having broken the father's authority and discipline, but they also do not want to have a milquetoast instead of a man.

Nieman-Marcus of Dallas, always with the first foot in the

fashion door, decided in 1957 that it was time to do something about the man in the family. The store invited all kinds of prominent people to a "fun fashion show" for men. Theatrical parties and lectures were organized, all "to Aim Appeal at the Forgotten Male." And this in Texas!

But the question is whether the tendency hasn't gone too far to be reversed. Dr. Otto von Mering, speaking to the Western Psychiatric Institute of the University of Pittsburgh in April, 1959, said: "Every father has to live with the idea of being the odd person. Since he can't rely on the old Victorian role, he must be happy as the odd-man out, co-existing as a third party."

In the current publications, the story of man's decline in America has changed from a trickle to a flood. "American wives are too bossy" says a doctor in *This Week Magazine*. *McCall's* felt it necessary in August, 1958, to run an article in defense of the "hen-pecked male." The long campaign in *McCall's* magazine on "Togetherness" was really an effort to popularize the idea "Welcome Home, Gentlemen!"

In the *New York Times*, April 1, 1959, a University of Wisconsin psychologist wanted to endow the man with a final feminine characteristic. He says that "fathers make better mothers than the mothers do . . . that it is entirely possible the woman may be replaced at home by the man." He further states: "The American male is physically endowed with all the really essential equipment to compete with the American female on equal terms in the rearing of infants."

Was this gentleman perhaps playing a little joke on us? Maybe not. The number of breast fed babies is steadily decreasing.

But while women are beginning to show some concern about what they are doing to their husbands, little attention is given to the position of the children. How about their sons? Husbands can defend themselves. But if a woman starts to put an apron on her son, and holds onto the strings, he's helpless. Perhaps nowhere do women use their power more recklessly than with their sons. It seems at first glance astonishing that they would dare to do this, but the flattery which their magazines dish out so generously has a lot to do with it. It makes them feel confident that they can do no wrong.

In every article, story, in every issue of women's magazines, there is a build-up of woman's authority, of her judgment. In the beginning Sara Josepha Hale did it cautiously, because the man of the house in her day would not have tolerated such an attitude. Edward Bok followed along, because of his profound admiration for his mother and grandmother, although his opinion of women was considerably tarnished before the end of his reign.

One of the articles in the Decalogue of American Beliefs is that women understand "human nature" better than men do. This agreeable notion has been richly fed by the goulash of second-rate psychiatry which has been ground out, not only by the women's magazines (let us be fair), but by every means of communication. To hold the interest of the casual reader this information has to be shallow and sensational. It avoids real knowledge that might really help a woman over a bad spot. Psychiatric information is risky when it's general; a small variation in a person's reactions may make a hash of the textbooks. Spilled out in the pages of magazines, it can be as dangerous as the old-fashioned patent medicines. Indeed, it is really a new kind of patent medicine.

So, there is a contradiction between the power women have and how they use it. The *Ladies' Home Journal,* October, 1959, claimed an average circulation of six million copies a month; *McCall's,* five and a half million; *Family Circle,* 5,121,124; *Good House-keeping,* 4,437,978; *Woman's Day,* 4,147,163; *Parents',* 1,811,389; *Seventeen,* 978,908; *Glamour,* 697,451; *Charm,* 657,335; *Mademoiselle,* 503,543.

It is true that many of the general women's magazines are not read by as many people as they used to be. It was customary to figure three-and-a-half readers for every copy during the 1930's. That figure has grown smaller. Even so, at the lowest estimate, this combined circulation reaches about thirty million women a month.

Thirty million women is a tremendous slice of the population. Their power as customers and consumers is overwhelming. Add to this their power as stockholders in corporations and one begins to sense how formidable a role they can and do play in the American way of life. Only in actual office holding has their power remained small. And there are ironies that have resulted from this rise to power; for instance, it is considered a news item when women share in the direction of banks and corporations, and sensational when they are chosen to head women's colleges.

Anyway, here they are, this strong, busy army of women who buy these magazines, who trust their editors; who let those editors tell them what is propaganda and what is truth. They are not stupid, far from it, and in matters where they know the background they are not credulous. But they never learned the background in history or politics, for instance. And so this army of women, like bees brewing a poisonous honey, is the Lady Persuaders who go out into the world and spread a confusion of lies, unhatched ideas, vanities and special pleadings.

It is almost unbelievably easy for special groups to plant propaganda in the women's magazines. There are several reasons for this. One is that the propaganda usually seems to be for something benevolent. Another is that many of the people pushing special interests are well-known and have good reputations. These impress the editors. And the editors themselves seem to use no real standard of measurement.

I do not for a moment say that women's magazines have been

all bad in their influence. They have been a vital asset in the spread of democracy among women. They have made woman's work easier in some ways. They have done a great deal in improving manners, although they have often been rather silly. They have done something to improve taste, though they emphasize the kind of taste that costs money, a "Keeping up with the Joneses," a rather tasteless business even if it is done with taste. They have also improved the serving of food, though with a tendency to rely on whipped cream and the cherry. But while they have made food preparation easier, and its service more agreeable, they have often had a devastating effect on its taste. *Good Housekeeping*, usually so sensible, in July, 1959, printed a recipe for lamb chop grill as follows: Mix roquefort with a teaspoon of Worcestershire, spread on chops.

Many of these magazines, especially the big ones, are losing sight of the pattern that built them up. One can almost see the wheels go round in the head of the editor. "Now, let's see," says the bright young brain, "women are interested in all kinds of things these days, so let's have a little of this and a little of that, some gossip and public affairs, but let's keep it lively (i.e., on the surface at least). Let's give them something they can talk about at the next card party."

> Something old,
> Something new,
> Something borrowed,
> But nothing blue!

Unfortunately the most popular subjects when women get together are still recipes, children's bright sayings, fashion, hair-dos and make-up. The magazines which remember this and proceed on that knowledge do continue strong.

At the time of this writing, the larger women's magazines—the "big three"—were all having difficulties. *McCall's* particularly had been slipping badly. The whole magazine field, men's and women's, was suffering from the competition of radio and television. But the women's general magazine field which had been so fertile for generations, was suffering more. Circulation was costing too much. Advertising tended to prefer special limited groups. Magazines like *Mademoiselle* have done better than the general magazines for women. And, of course, the store-distributed magazines, *Woman's Day* and *Family Circle,* which in a way are specialized too, have an immense advantage in savings on the cost of circulation, one of the largest items in magazine expense.

Meantime, though there are still millions of copies going out every month to women; each copy carrying exhortation and command to do this or that, all the way from trying out a new lipstick to trying out a new system of government; from a new way to cook cheese soufflé, to a new method of running the public schools. Perhaps this month's instructions are in direct contradiction to those of the month before. But what of that? The bright, gay amusing women are out in the world spreading what they read. Doesn't it make good conversation? And more than that, doesn't it make a woman feel that she is making the world a little better to live in?

But were they? Are they?

15

Question Period

An Editor who read this book has asked me some questions and I think perhaps it is only fair to write down his questions and my answers.

Do you think women are less intelligent than men?

No, I do not. The immense number of women who are doing a cool-headed job in business and the professions answers that question. However, among the women I know, hardly any ever reads a so-called "women's magazine."

There are plenty of men who are stupid or foolish. But on the whole, men are better trained and are likely to use their native brains to better effect. Given a man and a woman of equal native intelligence, the man will usually think better and more effectively than the woman and his interests are more impersonal. Also, men are more honest in talking to each other. From boyhood on they are used to being contradicted and put in their place. It still isn't good manners to contradict a woman. Some of this is cured by the business world, but not enough.

Do you mean to say that women shouldn't have the vote?

I think they *should* have the vote. In a democratic system they

are entitled to it. But I believe they should learn to look imper-
sonally on candidates and issues—they should know more about
what they're voting for or against.

What would you do about this ignorance?

Sister Margaret, a Roman Catholic teaching sister, who is the
head of Washington D. C.'s Trinity College, answered this. "The
mark of an educated woman is her use of leisure," she said. "Reading a book-of-the-month or seeing the latest play isn't enough.
Educated women must have definite views and standards. They
must know the good and the bad, and be able to say why. A
woman must not only know facts—she must have ideas about
them. The modern world needs more people—including girls—
who think for themselves." Of her own college she said: *"We are
not in the business of training committee women or bridge players."*

*Do you think women should stick to their kitchens, to their
households?*

Of course I do not. Why should they, unless they have small
children and no help? They could not keep busy there. The house
is seldom a full-time job any more. All the talk of whether women
should go out to work is academic. Women work because they
need money or because they have unused energy. Even in the old
days, when there were few short cuts to household labors, women
had to fill-in with useless embroideries and fancy work. Today
they may go out and take a job—and probably knit and sew too.

*Do you think the magazines have done a good job in changing
the American family?*

No, I do not. These magazines, all of them, have done a bad job
for one thing in spoiling the teenager. They have encouraged
women to use bits of information as conversation pieces. Some of
the magazines are still good on fashions, some on foods, but on
medicine and psychology they are, on the whole, shockingly bad.
Since they are published for large numbers of women, much of

the medical information has to be general, and, because of the nature of the publications, it has to have a news item aspect. Any doctor will tell you that most advance information about medicine and medical discoveries is unreliable. The very fact that it is news often indicates that it has not been properly tested. It takes years to test out medical discoveries.

As for the psychological material that they publish, here and there it is good, but usually it has the defect that any psychological study must have that is sprayed out to millions of people. It deals in ruinous half truths and oversimplifications.

Do you mean to say that men never base their votes on emotions?

No, but men manage better than women to keep their personal preferences and liking for good-looking girls out of their politics. Men at least try to figure out what they're voting for. And anyway, men's foolishness is amply taken care of in many places and women's, as related to their magazines, has been handled gingerly, if at all.

Isn't it true that modern theory believes that it is healthy in dealing with young people to be outspoken in matters of sex?

This, it seems to me, is entirely an individual problem—depending on the parents. In any case, I think that these magazines are not the place for such frankness, especially when, under all the pose of helping the poor kids, there is an enticement to excitement. The women's magazines use a mask of virtue with on-and-off protests of good intentions to commit the same offenses which they have attacked in others.

You do not like women's magazines, do you?

No, I do not. I have a high regard for the service material when it is good. I used to like to read the recipes and look at the fashions, but over-all they are a constant irritation. Mainly this is due to the pretense that the publication is a lofty, kindly, noble enterprise, when I know it is simply a business.

The big general magazines for women all lose money on their subscriptions. They reduce rates for short-term subscriptions; many let the subscriptions run on after they have expired, because the higher the circulation, the more advertisers are willing to pay (with some exceptions) to have their products displayed. Even the full price stated in the magazine doesn't cover the cost of its manufacture and distribution.

So, the advertisers pay the piper. Legitimately, the payer wants some piping done for the money he spends. He isn't spending his money for fun, but to sell a product. All that is reasonable and certainly good business, under the principle that both sides of a bargain should profit by it. But, then, why do the women's magazines keep harping on the theme that they are working always for the good of the reader? They choose cosmetics for *your* good, they run recipes for *your* good, they are positively lofty in the things they publish to help with *your* baby.

But have you ever seen any of the women's magazines give little bits of information like this . . . *for rough elbows or knees, the best and quickest cure is to rub them with a little wet salt. You can rub a roughened elbow for an hour with cold cream, but a minute with salt is more effective.*

But what advertising advantage is there in the sale of a spoonful of salt?

About the Author

This book grew naturally out of Helen Woodward's experience. It has been her good luck to know many of the people who have figured in the development of women's magazines in America. She has dealt with them on the inside as well as on the outside. Years ago she established special circulation departments for *Woman's Home Companion, Pictorial Review,* and *McCall's.* Later, as account executive for two leading advertising agencies, she bought space in the women's magazines. In Paris she worked with fashion periodicals to build up new styles in fabrics; she has written articles for them and sold them ideas.

After twenty years, Mrs. Woodward quit the advertising business because she wished to be free to travel with her husband, W. E Woodward, historian and biographer.

Ivan Obolensky, Inc.
New York, N. Y.